AFTER EFFECTS

Richard Harrington
Project Editor

CMP*Books*

San Francisco

Published by CMP Books

an imprint of CMP Media LLC

600 Harrison Street, San Francisco, CA 94107 USA

Tel: 415-947-6000; FAX: 415-947-6015

www.cmpbooks.com

email: books@cmp.com

Distributed to the book trade in the U.S. by:

Publishers Group West

1700 Fourth Street

Berkeley, CA 94710

1-800-788-3123

Distributed in Canada through:

Jaguar Book Group

100 Armstrong Avenue

Georgetown, Ontario M6K 3E7 Canada

905-877-4483

Printed in the United States of America

06 07 08 09 10   5 4 3 2 1

ISBN: 1-57820-267-1

CONTENTS

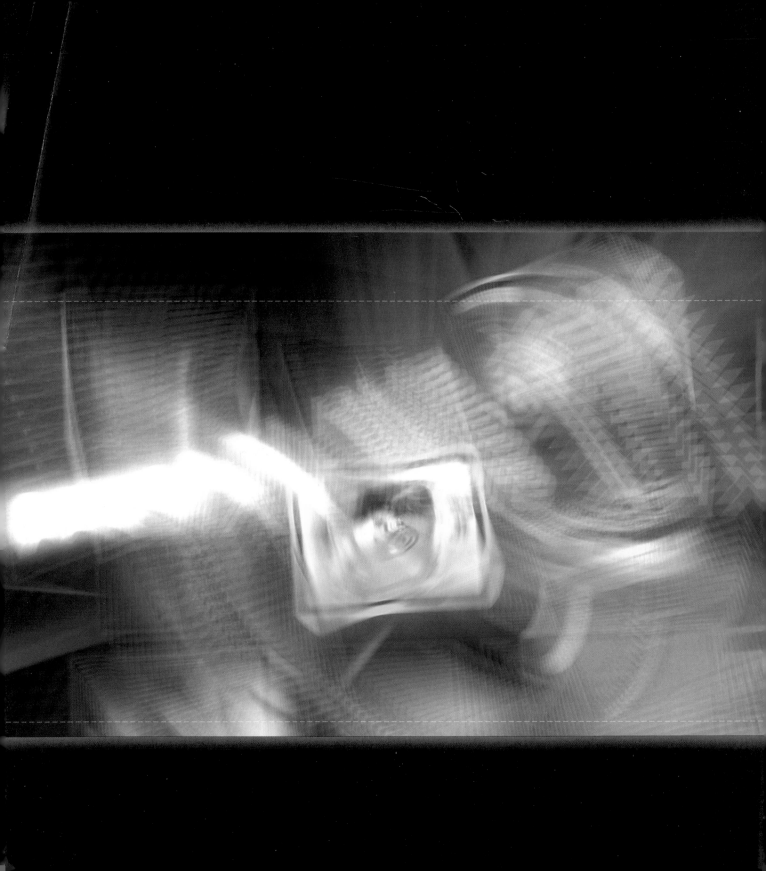

:: 01   :: 02   :: 03   :: 04   :: 05   :: 06   :: 07   :: 08   :: 09   :: 10   :: 11

FAST, WIDE AND 3D: XFX TRADE SHOW VIDEO

CHRIS AND TRISH MEYER, CYBERMOTION

When you're creating a web site or a brochure, you're assuming a person has come to you to read your information. When you create a commercial, you're assuming that the viewer will watch for all 30 seconds. But when someone is walking down an aisle at a trade show, you might have less than three seconds to grab their attention and lure them in. This was our challenge: creating a series of 30-second videos that conveyed a message, but just as important, encourage a person to stop, watch, and enter the booth to learn more.

For this project, our studio, CyberMotion was hired by CRISP (www.crispbranding.com), a boutique branding agency in Costa Mesa, California who can name the likes of Nestlé Foods and Coors Brewing among their clients. In this case, the client was XFX Technology, a leading maker of gaming video cards from China with a strong global presence, due in part to CRISP's rebranding. In this chapter, we will walk through some of the work we created for CRISP and XFX, discuss some of the considerations that went into it, and give you a detailed tutorial on how we created one of its main elements, framing devices for a number of low-res gaming videos.

WHAT'S ON THE DVD

The DVD contains the final video described in this chapter, as well as an After Effects project and sources to explore and recreate several elements of the video. Note that the sources have been copyrighted by CyberMotion, NVIDIA, VideoHelper, and XFX, and are not to be reused in any form.

01 » ELEMENTS FROM XFX'S PACKAGING,
INCLUDING THE CHARACTERS THAT
REPRESENTED EACH CARD FAMILY,
WERE TRANSLATED INTO THE LOOK
AND FEEL OF THE TRADE SHOW VIDEO.

Parameters

CRISP and XFX had four main themes to convey: Who We Are, How We Do It, What We Do, and a new product introduction. The catch was that the new product would not be ready in time for the first trade show, which was coming up in two weeks. Rather than create one continuous video, we decided to create four 30-second modules, linked together using logos of XFX and their main techn ology partner, chip company NVIDIA. Two modules would be created for the first trade show and are featured here.

The total budget was $10,000 plus expenses. CRISP and XFX had a number of print assets but no animated ones. Pure 3D animation can be costly and time-consuming to create, so we chose to use "real" 3D just for the XFX and NVIDIA. Logos we chose to build the rest in a psuedo-3D environment inside After Effects. We drew on our extensive stock footage library for the backgrounds, and downloaded videos from NVIDIA. Beyond that, the main hero was the text, and the messages it conveyed.

Music Spotting

When audio and the visuals are closely tied together, they feed off of each other, heightening the impact of the work. Therefore, we strongly encourage our clients to choose the music before we get started with animation.

One of our favorite stock music houses is VideoHelper. Their music has a strong attitude, with numerous clear "hit points" and sections for us to key off of. We pointed CRISP to VideoHelper's web site (www.videohelper.com) to audition and select music, CRISP passed along URLs of candidates to XFX in China, which is much faster than overnighting CDs around the world.

Much stock music is composed around the "three movement" framework common in symphonies: a fast introduction, a slow middle section, and a fast conclusion that recapitulates themes from the first movement. CRISP found a couple of pieces that had 30 second first and third movements (each matching the length of one of our modules), with quiet bridges (great for the logo section, helping to tie the modules together). After selection, we then "spotted" the music to get an idea of how many major sections there were, and where the hit points and individual beats were falling. This is the skeleton or grid around which we start to build our animations.

⚙ CUSTOMIZING STOCK FOOTAGE

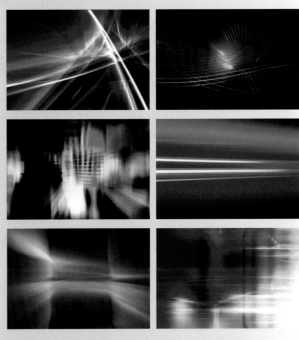

» WE COMBINED ELEMENTS FROM ARTBEATS' DREAMLIGHT AND LIGHT ALCHEMY COLLECTIONS, DIGITAL VISION'S ATMOSPHERICS, ELECTRO, AND LIGHTFORMS, AND GETTY IMAGES' SYNERGY: HYPERVISION LIBRARIES TO CREATE OUR BACKGROUNDS.

There are a large number of excellent stock footage libraries of abstract backgrounds available. Using these can save a lot of time and money. The challenge with stock footage is making sure it is appropriate to the client's job and making it look different than someone else who has the same library.

After discussing the desired "vibe" with CRISP, we selected a number of images we thought might work, and narrowed them down with their input. We then layered and crossfaded between different combinations of these clips, using a variety of blending modes. The resulting composites were colorized to match XFX's logo and packaging colors using the Boris BCC Tritone plug-in.

 All of our libraries were of the NTSC D1 size of 720x486 pixels with a 4:3 aspect ratio, while for this job we needed a PAL 16:9 aspect size of 1024x576 pixels. This required scaling up the footage by as much as 160 percent. Fortunately, we could live with the resulting softness, as we wanted our backgrounds to "sit back" from the text and other foreground elements; pursuing a hot, glowing look made their softness seem appropriate. We also conformed the frame rate of all the footage to match PAL's speed of 25 fps.

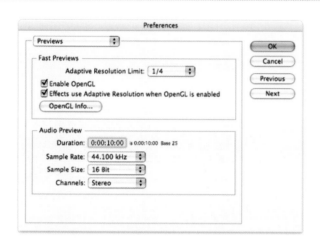

02 » TO AUDITION 10 SECONDS OF THE SOUNDTRACK AT A TIME, SET THE
AUDIO PREVIEW DURATION TO 10:00 IN REFERENCES>PREVIEWS.

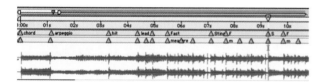

03 » WE USE LAYER MARKERS TO SPOT IMPORTANT EVENTS IN A
SOUNDTRACK. TO CREATE A LAYER MARKER, SELECT THE LAYER AND
PRESS * (ASTERISK KEY) ON THE NUMERIC KEYPAD. TO ADD A NAME
WHEN YOU CREATE IT, HOLD DOWN OPTION (ALT) BEFORE PRESSING *.

Open this chapter's example project, CyberMotion_XFX.aep, and then in the Project window double-click the comp 01a-music spotting to see our result. Use the – or = keys to zoom in the Timeline window until you see about 10 seconds of time. If the audio waveform is not visible, select the layer VH023_52 (our shorthand for VideoHelper disc 23, track 52) and type LL to reveal it. Open Preferences>Previews and set the Audio Preview Duration to 10:00. (SEE FIGURE 02.)

Press Home, and then press . (period key) on the numeric keypad to audition the first 10 seconds of the music. While listening, watch the cursor move through time, relating what you hear to the spikes you see in the audio waveform. In the Timeline window, observe how we've noted the beats with unnamed layer markers, and the starts of new measures of music with the markers that have the letter "m." We added a second silent, invisible layer to help us mark different sections of the music, such as F for Fast and S for Sting. Press any key to stop the preview; then move the time marker down the timeline to audition other sections of the music. (SEE FIGURE 03.)

After spotting the music, we did a timing test to make sure all of the desired words and phrases would fit, with enough time to digest each thought. This allowed us to fine-tune the messaging with CRISP and XFX. To see one of these tests, open comp 01b-timed text and press 0 on the numeric keypad to RAM Preview it.

PREVIEW A SEGMENT

To preview a segment of the final movie, press a number such as 1 (on the standard keyboard, not the numeric keypad) to jump to that marker, press B to set the start of the work area to that point, press a later number such as 2 to jump to that marker, press E to end the work area, and then press 0 on the numeric keypad to RAM Preview that segment. You can also use Page Up and Page Down to step through the piece frame by frame.

The Final Work: Dissected

Selecting music and finalizing the wording took one of the two weeks we had in the schedule. All of the remaining animation was completed in five days. Let's examine the finished piece, and discuss some of their major sections.

In the Project window double-click the composition 02_final piece to open it. If you have not already viewed the finished piece on the book's DVD, hold down Option (Alt) and double-click the layer XFX.mov to open it in a QuickTime player window, press the spacebar to preview it.

Close the QuickTime window when done and turn your attention to the Timeline window. We've added layer markers describing some of the sections, as well as comp markers for easy location of specific examples.

Following is what to look for at each comp marker.

0: On the first hit in the music, we introduce the XFX logo, and zoom it back in space to anchor the background. To create the logo, we took Illustrator artwork provided by CRISP, extruded it with the Zaxwerks 3D Invigorator for After Effects Pro plug-in, and exported a 3D model. We surfaced, lit, and animated the model in Electric Image Animation System. (SEE FIGURE 04.)

1: We bring on the first text element, tumble it, and switch out the text to the second message in the middle of the tumble. GenArts'S_GlowEdges effect is used on the text here and extensively throughout the piece to add a bright haze around elements.

04 » THE 3D XFX LOGO OPENS THE PIECE, ZOOMING BACK TO ANCHOR THE BACKGROUND.

05 » THE CARD DANCE EFFECT IS USED TO DYNAMICALLY ASSEMBLE AND BLOW UP THE SIGNATURE CHARACTERS PLUS VIDEO

06 » THE MIXTURE OF
BACKGROUND LAYERS
EVOLVES AS EACH NEW
PHRASE APPEARS.

2: For "hero" shots, we had still images of the characters from the packaging, plus demo videos from NVIDIA. To give them a sense of 3D space and add some mystery, they are assembled and disassembled using the Simulation>Card Dance effect. Study the comp 03_Card Wipe for an example of this animation. (SEE FIGURE 05.)

3: Note that as we swap in different messaging phrases, we keep changing the mix of background elements, while keeping them unified by tinting them all with XFX and NVIDIA's signature radiation-green (using Boris BCC Tritone). (SEE FIGURE 06.)

4: The "quiet" middle section is dedicated to displaying the XFX and NVIDIA logos. Rather than use a single continuous shot, to maintain interest we animated multiple camera passes on the logos in Electric Image, and then edited between them in time with the music. The light rays are created using Trapcode's Shine plug-in. (SEE FIGURE 07.)

5: Use the Page Up and Page Down keys to move before and after this point in time. We covered some of our hard cuts by compositing film flashes from Artbeats' Film Clutter library on top of our footage, using Add mode. The colorful randomness of exposed film creates more excitement than using a simple white solid. Similar flashes are used at 52:24 and 57:04. (SEE FIGURE 08.)

07 » MULTIPLE MOVES ON THE 3D LOGOS ARE EDITED TO CHANGE IN TIME WITH THE MUSIC.

⚙ **FROM .WMV TO .MOV**

Some of NVIDIA's demo movies were posted online using the Windows Media Viewer format (.wmv) files. After Effects cannot import this type of file. We opened them on a Windows XP computer using Microsoft's free Windows Media Encoder and saved them as .avi files. We then converted them to QuickTime .mov files to make them easier to handle on the Mac.

The section after this marker includes a number of NVIDIA demos framed and being flown about in 3D space. Later, we will break down how we built this.

6: To emphasize the high-pitched guitar stings in the music, we tumbled the logos extremely fast, with Motion Blur enabled. Trapcode's Shine was used to brighten and glow these tumbles. We used the distraction to swap out the text in the middle of each sting. (SEE FIGURE 09.)

7: We borrowed the arrangement of the NVIDIA demo videos and applied it to third-party partner logos. When you have too many logos or words to get on screen in a limited period of time, one of our answers is to put them all on all the time, arrayed in 3D space. As there was not time nor budget to rebuild all of these logos as 3D models, we applied Perspective>Bevel Alpha to give some illusion of thickness. (SEE FIGURE 10.)

08 » FLASHES FROM THE ARTBEATS FILM CLUTTER LIBRARIES ADD EXCITEMENT WHILE CONCEALING HARD CUTS IN THE VIDEO.

09 » AN ARRAY OF VIDEO SCREENS TUMBLED EXTREMELY FAST–WITH MOTION BLUR–ACTS AS ANOTHER EYE GRABBER.

10 » THIRD-PARTY PARTNER LOGOS WERE ALSO
        ARRAYED IN SPACE AS AN ECHO OF THE VIDEO
        SCREENS IN THE PREVIOUS SECTION.

8: The desire is to keep building energy towards the end. For the final pieces of messaging, we added a nervous quality by having them bounce randomly by applying a "wiggle" expression to their Position parameter: wiggle(1.8181, 5). The first number, the number of wiggles per second, was carefully chosen so they would bounce in time with the music. The second number is how many pixels they wiggle. An additional trick is that we used two copies of the text: one that "stuck" in position, and another that continues to fly off screen. This is demonstrated in the comp 04_energy text. (SEE FIGURE 11.)

9: The final gaming logo was also created using Zaxwerks' 3D Invigorator Pro and blown up in Electric Image using their plug-in Mr. Nitro. The pieces you see whizzing about are actual facets of the model. This reveals the XFX logo, which was the first element we saw at the start. (SEE FIGURE 12.)

11 » TWO COPIES OF THE TEXT STREAK ON.
        ONE STICKS IN POSITION, WHILE THE OTHER
        STREAKS OFF.

12 » THE FINAL LOGO WAS BLOWN UP IN ELECTRIC IMAGE USING THE MR. NITRO PLUG-IN.

Exercise: Framing Video

We were fortunate that XFX's technology partner NVIDIA posts online lots of demonstration videos showing what their chips can do, and posts them online. Using these proved much easier than clearing videos from individual games. Unfortunately, most of these videos were small and heavily compressed, ruling out playing them full-screen. As an alternative, we decided to have several videos on screen at once, so we could make each one small and sharp.

Raw videos floating in space aren't very sexy so we decided to suspend the videos in interesting frames. The budget didn't allow for creating elaborate frames in a 3D program so we decided to create simple frames inside After Effects. Here's how you can do the same:

1: Choose a Composition> New Composition. In the Composition Settings dialog, set the size to 360x280 (slightly larger than the 320x240 video provided), using square pixels, and set the Resolution to Full. Pick a sensible name such as "my frame," enter a Duration of 10:00, and click OK. (SEE FIGURE 13.)

2: Along the bottom edge of the Comp window, enable the Toggle View Masks switch, as well as Toggle Transparency Grid. (SEE FIGURE 14.)

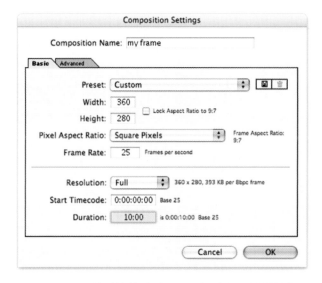

13 » CREATE A NEW COMPOSITION SLIGHTLY LARGER THAN THE VIDEO YOU NEED TO FRAME.

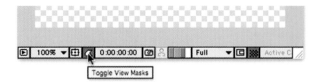

14 » ENABLE THE COMP WINDOW'S TOGGLE VIEW MASKS AND TOGGLE TRANS-PARENCY GRID. THESE BUTTONS APPEAR DARKER WHEN ENABLED.

3: In this comp, add a Layer>New>Solid. Name it "frame," click on the Make Comp Size button, and give it a strong color. Then click New. (SEE FIGURE15.)

4: With your FRAME layer highlighted, select Layer>Mask>New Mask. This creates a mask the shape of your solid. Type MM to reveal your mask's parameters in the Timeline window. Click on the word Shape on the same line as the parameter Mask Shape in the Timeline window. Edit the values to inset the Bounding Box

10 to 20 pixels on all sides by adding to the Left and Top values and subtracting from the Right and Bottom values. You should see the checkerboard grid in the Comp window wherethe solid is transparent. (SEE FIGURE 16.)

5: Change the popup in the Switches/Modes column from Add to Subtract; this will cut the center out of your solid. (SEE FIGURE 17.)

15 » CREATE A NEW SOLID THE SAME SIZE AS YOUR COMPOSITION.

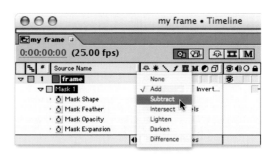

17 » SET MASK 1 TO SUBTRACT ITS SHAPE FROM THE SOLID, MAKING THE CENTER TRANSPARENT. USE THE PEN TOOL TO ADD MORE POINTS TO YOUR MASK.

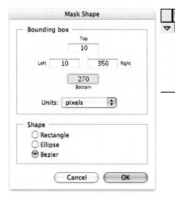

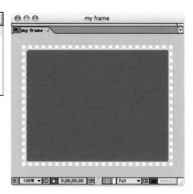

16 » CREATE A NEW MASK, AND EDIT THE MASK SHAPE'S BOUNDING BOX, IN SETTING IT 10 TO 20 PIXELS ON ALL SIDES.

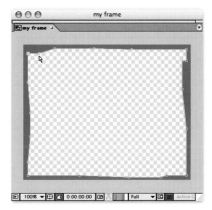

18 » USE THE PEN TOOL TO ADD MORE POINTS
TO YOUR MASK.

6: Now edit the mask shape to make your frame more interesting.
Press G to select the Pen tool. Click along your mask shape to
add more vertices to your mask. For starters, try adding four
points to each side. Make sure a "+" symbol is visible next to
the pen cursor before you click; otherwise, After Effects will
think you want to start drawing a new mask. If needed, choose
Undo to remove accidental mask points. (SEE FIGURE 18.)

7: Press V to return to the Selection tool. In your sets of four extra
mask points, Shift+click or drag a marquee to select the inner two.
Then use the cursor keys to nudge them to a new position, creating a more detailed shape for the frame. Nudge the other points
as needed. Do this for each side of the frame. (SEE FIGURE 19.)

8: Now inset the video in the middle of your frame. In the Project
window, twirl open the Sources>Video folder. Select one of the
NVIDIA clips, and type Command+/ (Control+/) to add it to the
middle of your comp.

At this point, you can edit, add, or delete mask points to create a
more interesting relationship between the frame and video. You
can either make "spars" that connect the frame to the video, or
leave the video floating in the middle of the frame. (SEE FIGURE
20.)

9: To add apparent thickness to your frame, select it and add
Effect>Perspective>Bevel Alpha. If you like, do the same to
the video. In the Effect Controls window, optionally increase the
Edge Thickness to make the bevel more obvious.

19 » NUDGE YOUR NEW MASK POINTS TO CREATE INTERESTING
CUT-OUTS AND EXTENSIONS TO YOUR FRAME.

20 » ADD A VIDEO TO THE MIDDLE OF THE COMP AND FURTHER TWEAK THE
FRAME'S SHAPE.

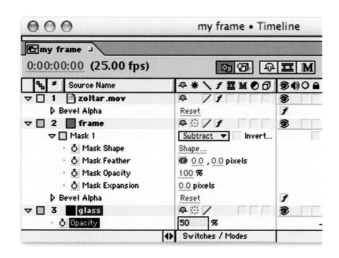

10: We like to add a "backing glass" to fill in the gaps between the frame and video while still being able to see bits of objects behind. Type Command+Y (Control+Y) to create another new solid. Make sure it is the same size as the comp, but this time change its color to black, and change its name to "glass." Click OK. Then type Command+Shift+[(Control+Shift+[) to send it to the bottom of the layer stack.

11: With the glass layer still selected, type T to reveal its Opacity setting. Scrub its value in the Timeline window while watching the Comp window, looking for the checkerboard pattern to appear in the "glass" areas, somewhere around 50 percent to 65 percent works well. (SEE FIGURE 21.)

21 » TO GIVE THE ILLUSION OF SEMITRANSPARENT GLASS, PLACE A BLACK SOLID IN THE BACKGROUND AND REDUCE ITS OPACITY.

23 » WE ARRAYED A NUMBER OF THESE FRAMED VIDEOS IN 3D SPACE, CONNECTED THEM TO A CENTRAL NULL OBJECT, AND ANIMATED THE NULL.

In the project window, double-click the comp 05_our frame to see a slightly fancier frame we created for the XFX project. We used two mask shapes: the inner frame pattern was subtracted from an outer rounded-corner mask (created with Profound Effects Useful Assistants). **(SEE FIGURE 22.)**

After creating one frame, we followed the old artistic adage of "repeat, but with variations," creating new compositions with frames for the other videos. In some cases the variations were simple rotations or flips of the original mask shape.

We then added these frame precomps to a master comp, and arranged them in a grid in 3D space, leaving semi-random holes to create interest through unpredictability. However, if you look closely, you will notice that we arranged the front row of video frames in an "X" to reinforce the company name. These precomps were attached to a central Null Object, which was then animated in space to move towards and away from a camera, changing direction as if being bounced around by the music. **(SEE FIGURE 23.)**

Open the comp 02_final piece again, and preview the section between comp markers 5 and 7. You will notice that we performed some other subtle tricks, such as making the videos semi-transparent, changing the arrangement of the frames halfway through, subduing the color of the frames in the back plane to make them recede into space, and editing the videos here and there to better match the music.

22 » FOR THE XFX VIDEO, WE CREATED SLIGHTLY FANCIER FRAMES WITH ROUNDED EDGES BY USING TWO MASK SHAPES.

24 » IN DVD STUDIO PRO, USE THE INSPECTOR TO SET
THE DISC'S FIRST PLAY AND THE TRACK'S END JUMP
BOTH TO BE YOUR VIDEO.

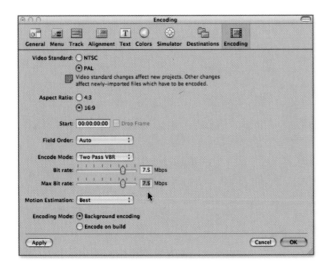

25 » REMEMBER TO SET THE ENCODING PREFERENCES TO
THE CORRECT VIDEO STANDARD AND ASPECT RATIO,
WITH THE DESIRED DATA RATE TO MAXIMIZE QUALITY.

DVD Considerations

The delivery requirements for this job were a bit unusual: a widescreen PAL DVD that would auto-start upon insertion and con-
tinuously loop. On most jobs, we hand off DVD authoring to those
who specialize in it, but to keep the costs down we agreed to do
the authoring ourselves.

We normally use Apple's iDVD when creating simple DVD proofs
for clients. However, iDVD does not support autoplay or looping,
so we stepped up to Apple's DVD Studio Pro. The trick to having
a disc play on insertion is to set the disc's First Play to be your
video track; to get it to loop, also set the track's End Jump to this
same track. (SEE FIGURE 24.)

As the discs had to be delivered overseas for a trade show on
a tight deadline, and we didn't have a PAL format DVD player
or monitor of our own to test the final disc with (and again, the
budget would not accommodate these purchases), we wanted to
make our production process as bulletproof as possible by tak-
ing decisions out of DVD Studio Pro's hands. For example, if you
render a normal 720x576 PAL frame in After Effects, there is
ambiguity over whether this is a normal 4x3 aspect ratio movie,
or a 16x9 aspect ratio movie that has an "anamorphic squeeze"
to cram the widescreen image into a normal PAL frame. Therefore, we rendered at the full square-pixel 1024x768 widescreen
size and handed that off to DVD Studio Pro to compress. To
ensure that the movie will be treated as PAL video, remember
to set the Encoding preferences before you import your movie.
(SEE FIGURE 25.)

Field order was also another area of concern. PAL can be upper
field first (professional D1-spec video) or lower field first (DV),

even for the same frame size. Different software packages also define upper, lower, first, second, even, and odd fields in different ways. We also knew that the DVD may be played back on computers, which do not correctly represent fields. Therefore, we decided to frame-render the movie. This was as much an aesthetic decision as a technical one, as frame rendering results in more motion blur than field rendering for the same Shutter Angle in After Effects. The final 25fps progressive-scan video has more dreamlike motion akin to 24fps film.

After we burned a test disc, we were not satisfied with the quality; there was visible banding or posterization around the "light ray" effects and with some of the layered background images. One partial cure was increasing the bit rate settings in DVD Studio Pro's Encoding dialog. As we were trying to fit only a few minutes onto an entire DVD, file size was not an issue, so we set both the Bit Rate and Max Bit Rate as high as we could. Although a DVD's maximum bit rate is 9Mbps, you need to leave room for audio, control tracks, and to recover from inevitable drop-outs. The suggested maximum in the real world is 7.5Mps.

However, even this did not cure all of our problems; nor did setting After Effects to 16bpc (bit per channel) color depth. The next corrective action was adding some noise to break up the banding patterns. For the problematic backgrounds, we placed an Adjustment Layer on top of the composite and applied Effect>Noise & Grain>Noise HLS Auto, with noise in the Hue channel set to 1 percent. **(SEE FIGURE 26.)**

For the light rays, we duplicated our source layer, and applied Trapcode's Shine to the duplicate. On top of this we placed stock footage of blowing and drifting smoke (from the Artbeats ReelFire and ReelExplosions libraries), applied Effect>Adjust Levels to

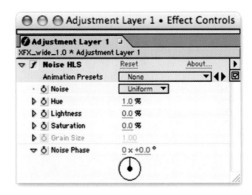

26 » A SLIGHT AMOUNT OF NOISE IN THE HUE CHANNEL BROKE UP BANDING PROBLEMS THAT APPEARED DURING ENCODING.

VCD

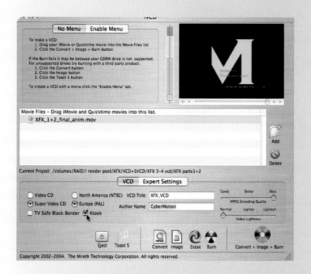

» MIRETH'S IVCD PROVIDES AN EASY WAY TO CREATE VIDEO CDS,
WHICH ARE POPULAR IN SOME ASIAN COUNTRIES.

A popular format in some Asian countries is Video CD (VCD). This places a few minutes of MPEG-encoded video on a CD instead of a DVD. As part of our deliverables, we were asked to create both VCD and SVCD (Super VCD) discs.

We used the inexpensive VCD and SVCD creator iVCD from Mireth Technology (www.mireth.com). Although VCDs don't have nearly the interactive programming potential of DVDs (and are of much lower visual quality, by the way), they do have autoplay and looping functions, which are exactly what we needed for this job. iVCD refers to this as "kiosk" mode. iVCD also automatically letterboxed our widescreen video for playback in VCD's 4:3 aspect ratio format.

maximize its brightness and contrast, and used this as a luminance matte for the light rays to help break them up. Again, this choice was driven by aesthetics as much as technical requirements: Matting light rays with noise, smoke, and similar textures gives them a much more mysterious air. A split-screen of a similar effect is set up for you to study in comp 06_mysterious rays. This composition uses the Professional edition's Fractal Noise effect, as well Cycore's CC Radial Blur. **(SEE FIGURE 27.)**

The final DVD authoring consideration is simple, but significant: Some older DVD players can take up to a second to get playback running properly. It is suggested that for maximum compatibility you should insert a second of black and silence at the head of your files. The movie also ends in black, so the loop point–where the video would otherwise be frozen–will appear seamless.

Mission: Accomplished

We feel the final result was fast, loose, and fun. This video's first use was at the huge CeBIT convention in Germany, and XFX's English distributor reported it was a resounding success. And from our own point of view, it was fun to create a video where you loosen the tie and display a lot of attitude, rather than worry about painting well inside the lines.

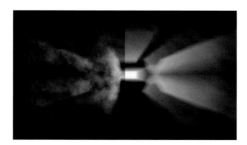

27 » THIS SPLIT SCREEN LIGHT RAY SHOWS THE VISUAL
BENEFITS OF USING A SMOKY OR CLOUDY TEXTURE
AS A LUMINANCE MATTE FOR LIGHT-RAY EFFECTS.

ABOUT THE AUTHORS

Chris and Trish Meyer are the creative forces behind CyberMotion, and award-winning motion graphics studio in Los Angeles. They have animated television and film opening tiles (including The Talented Mr. Ripley and Cold Mountain) for NBC, ABC, HBO, Fox, TLC, New Line, Paramount, and others. They also mix in a good amount of corporate work, creating trade show videos plus graphics for training, sales, and publicity materials for companies ranging from Apple to Xerox. CyberMotion has also contributed imagery for such unusual venues as a nine-screen CircleVision exhibit at the Korean Expo and the four-block-long Fremont Street Experience in Las Vegas.

CyberMotion's studio contains eight computers for the two artists–seven Macs and one Windows XP box–connected by a peer-to-peer gigabit Ethernet network. Their main workstations are dual-processor Apple G5s driving 22" Cinema displays; for video previewing, both also have Blackmagic Design DeckLink cards connected to 20" Sony monitors. Their main application is Adobe After Effects (for which they were one of the original development sites) with a wide variety of plug-ins. They also use Adobe Photoshop and Illustrator, Apple Final Cut Pro and Motion, Maxon Cinema 4D, Electric Image Universe, Digidesign Pro Tools, Ableton Live, and a number of small utilities.

Trish and Chris Meyer are respected authors, writing the Motion Graphics column for DV magazine and several highly regarded books on After Effects: the Creating Motion Graphics series, and After Effects in Production. Chris also currently sits of the Broadcast Designers Association's Board of Governors.

FURTHER READING

Creating Motion Graphics with After Effects, Volumes 1 and 2
by Trish & Chris Meyer
(CMP Books 2004, 2005)

After Effects in Production
by Trish & Chris Meyer (CMP Books 2005)

DVD Authoring and Production
by Ralph LaBarge (CMP Books 2001)

DVD Studio Pro 2 Solutions
by Erica Sadun (Sybex 2004)

DVD Studio Pro Visual QuickPro Guide
by Marin Sitter (Peachpit Press 2004)

MESA CHANNEL 11

PROGRAM GUIDE   FRIDAY, MARCH 18

6:00 AM - Traffic Check

8:00 AM - Senator Kyl's Report to
                Arizona

8:30 AM - Covering Mesa - Ride Choice

8:36 AM - Covering Mesa - Rec 'n Roll

8:41 AM - Covering Mesa - Light Rail
                Groundbreaking

8:49 AM - Covering Mesa - Growing Great
                Neighborhoods

AUTOMATING ANIMATED GRAPHICS:
MESA CHANNEL 11 PROGRAM GUIDE

GLEN STEPHENS, PIXEL POST STUDIOS, LLC

Using Photoshop and After Effects to create a program guide animation that automatically updates for daily programming changes.

When you mention After Effects and Photoshop, most designers think of them as tools for creating motion elements for video projects, compositing, show opens, and similar uses. But rarely do you think of them as tools that can run unattended to build dynamic content for broadcast delivery. This is how I used these tools to create a system for a cable station in Arizona.

The challenge was to create an animation of a program guide that would scroll for 45 seconds with the programming schedule for that day. The animation would need to be automatically recreated every day for the programming content on that day. This animation would serve the purpose of telling viewers what time different shows would air throughout the day. Many networks such as E! Entertainment, MTV Networks, and Comedy Central use a similar approach but give programming information only at the end of a show for the next two to three hours. Because our approach needed to be as automated as possible, we went with the idea that it would be best to give the entire day's schedule at the top of every hour since viewers frequently need to know what aired earlier in the day as well as upcoming programming.

THIS CHAPTER COVERS
a solution that works only on the Mac OS. Apple-Script plays a heavy role in how this solution works, and AppleScript is not available on the Windows operating system. It is possible to achieve the same results using VBScript, but that will not be covered.

WHAT'S ON THE DVD
The DVD contains the final video described in this chapter, as well as the Photoshop files, After Effects project and source files, the FileMaker Pro database, the PHP file, and the AppleScript files. Note that the sources are copyright Mesa Channel 11, VideoHelper, and are not to be reused in any form.

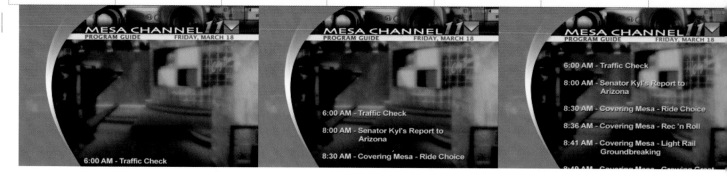

Parameters

The animation required music, text specific to the day's programming, and the day and date spelled out in the animation. The text needed to scroll from bottom to top, and the amount of content in a given day's programming schedule would vary, so the animation needed to be dynamically adjusted to fit the content perfectly in the 45-second time frame of the animation. The final project needed to be built in such a way that it didn't require any staff involvement to be created each day. The final product needed to dynamically get the programming information, build the animation, and upload it to the playback server so the next day when the animation ran, it would display the current day's information. Because of the time commitment already made by the staff, it was imperative that this all happen without staff involvement.

Technologies and Tools

There are a number of technologies and software solutions that were used to tie all of the elements of this project together. I will cover some in great detail while only mentioning resources for others. Here is a list of all of the various technologies and tools that were used to make it all work.

1. After Effects
2. Photoshop
3. JavaScript
4. AppleScript
5. FileMaker Pro
6. PHP
7. MySQL
8. XML

Project Phases

There were three phases in getting this project completed.

1. Designing the look of the final piece, which included creating the elements in Photoshop, and animating them in After Effects, where the music is also added to the animation.

2. Acquiring the programming data in a database.

3. Automating the daily process of building the animation with day-specific data.

The timeline for this project was approximately two weeks. The initial graphic design phase only took a few days to lock down. The majority of the time was spent writing the scripts that would control the system and running tests to make sure that all of the formatting was correct and that everything worked regardless of changing variables.

Before we go into detail on how I achieved each phase, let's look at the general workflow for the project and how each technology fit into the puzzle.

By following the flowchart in illustration 1, you can see that our programming information is in a MySQL database on an XServe G5 server. Because I decided to use FileMaker Pro to automate this system, I needed to get the data from MySQL into FileMaker. The easiest and fastest way to do this is by importing the data as XML. I wrote a PHP script that would create the XML that FileMaker needed to import our show information, which consisted of date, time, and show title. The PHP file that was used is included on the DVD. You can also see a live version of the XML by visiting www.mesachannel11.com/guide.php.

The FileMaker database was programmed to automatically import the programming information from the MySQL database at 1 A.M. every morning. Once it had the programming info, it needed to format the data and prepare it to be passed to Photoshop. Once the

programming information was formatted for that particular day, the FileMaker database would send this information to Photoshop to build the template of the scroll. Because Photoshop supports scripting, the formatted text data was sent using AppleScript directly from FileMaker to text layers in Photoshop. Once Photoshop had the day's information in the text layers, the file is saved and closed, again using AppleScript calls from FileMaker. After the Photoshop file was updated, File-Maker would call an AppleScript that would open the After Effects project that had the layers from the Photoshop file, music, and animation set in a composition. Because After Effects brings in and applies any changes made to Photoshop files, the After Effects project now has all of the current data to scroll. After Effects, being less scriptable than Photoshop, required Java Script to tell it to render a particular comp. However, in order to get that JavaScript command to After Effects, I had to use AppleScript yet again to send the Java Script command to After Effects. Once the daily movie was rendered, AppleScript closed the After Effects project without saving the changes, and then a final AppleScript was used to upload the rendered movie to the playback server and then delete it from the local machine. Although it may sound tough, hang in there. You'll be able to integrate some (or even all) of these techniques into your workflow.

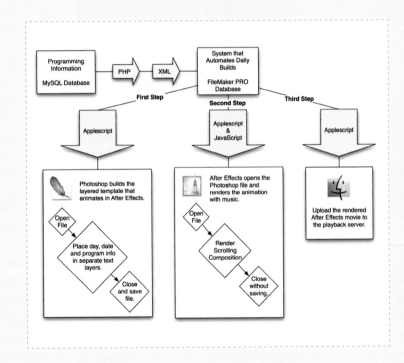

02 » STILL FRAME FROM FINAL PROJECT

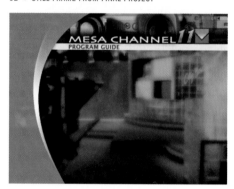

03 » BACKGROUND IMAGE WITHOUT DYNAMIC TEXT

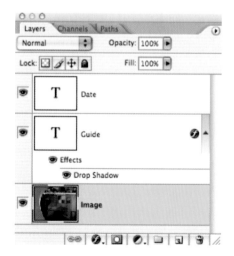

04 » LAYERS OF PHOTOSHOP FILE WITH DYNAMIC TEXT

Phase 1: Designing the Look

:: PHOTOSHOP

The design aspect of the project, the style, and how it would look was done in Photoshop. The graphic designer I worked with was given the parameters for creating a full-page graphic with the necessary information that was branded to the station. It needed to include a large body area for the scroll, the name of the station, and the date. **(SEE FIGURE 02.)**

Once the look of the scroll was finalized, a flattened version of the background was saved without any text elements that would change from day to day. This flattened file was used to create the Photoshop file that FileMaker would update daily and that After Effects would render. **(SEE FIGURE 03.)**

The Photoshop file that is dynamically updated each day is a fairly basic file. There are only two text layers and a layer of the composite background created previously. The first text layer is for the date, and the second text layer is for the programming information that is going to scroll. **(SEE FIGURE 04.)**

There are three important factors when creating a Photoshop template file that will be modified using a script.

1. All text elements need to be on separate layers.

2. All text layers need to have the correct fonts, colors, layer styles, and text alignment set so that everything looks correct as the text changes.

3. Once text layers are created, they need to be manually re-named. This is due to the fact that Photoshop automatically names text layers based on the text contained within the layer. If you don't manually override the automatic name, then the name of the layer will change each time the text in the layer is changed.

Because our script will call a specific layer by name to change its text, the name needs to stay the same from version to version.

You will notice that the text in the Guide layer extends below the boundary of the canvas. **(SEE FIGURE 05.)**

This is OK, because After Effects will read the entire layer and will not constrain it to the canvas size. This gives you the tall text layer that you need to scroll. To make sure that the scrolling keyframes are correct when we get to After Effects, it is important to place sample text in the Guide layer so that it will be approximately the same length that it will be when it is built each day.

:: AFTER EFFECTS

Importing the Photoshop File

Once the Photoshop template file is done, it is time to make it move in After Effects, add some fades to and from black, and add our music. From here I created a new project in After Effects. The Photoshop file needs to be imported as a composition, and the footage dimension need to be set to Layer Size. **(SEE FIGURE 06.)**

This is what will allow After Effects to read in the entire height of the scrolling text in our Guide layer. Setting it to Document Size would crop the text to only what is visible on the canvas.

Building the Scroll

There is now a comp called Program Guide comp 1. This composition is where all of the keyframes will be added to animate the scroll. The first thing you will notice is that because we created our drop shadow in Photoshop, there is an additional layer in our comp that is the drop shadow of the text. This drop shadow layer needs to be parented to the Guide layer so that as we scroll the text, the drop shadow will follow. **(SEE FIGURE 07.)**

Now we need to create the appearance that the text scrolls in

05 » THE TEXT IN THE GUIDE LAYER EXTENDS BELOW THE CANVAS BOUNDARY

06 » AFTER EFFECTS IMPORT DIALOG SETTINGS

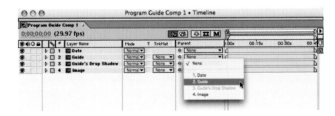

07 » PARENT THE DROP SHADOW LAYER TO THE TEXT LAYER.

08 » MASK THE HEADER OF THE GRAPHIC

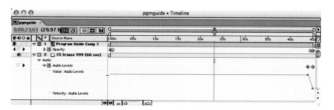

10 » AUDIO KEYFRAMES THAT FADE OUT MUSIC

09 » KEYFRAMES FOR SCROLLING TEXT POSITION

front of the bottom portion of the background but behind the header portion. We accomplish this by duplicating the Image layer in the comp and moving it below the Date layer. This new layer now needs to be masked to the size of the header. Using the rectangular mask tool, I drew a mask around the header portion. **(SEE FIGURE 08.)**

Now it is time to create the keyframes for the crawl. First, I positioned the Guide layer text just below the bottom of the screen edge and created a position keyframe at 00:00:00:00. I then created a second position keyframe at the end of the 45-second comp and positioned the text where it needed to be at the end of the scroll. Knowing that the length of the scroll for each day could vary, I created the After Effects file using sample text that was the average length that the programming text would be and then positioned it so that it would end just as it scrolled off the screen. This is so that if the text is shorter on a given day, there will only be a second or two where the text has scrolled completely off screen, and for text on days that is slightly longer, the end of the scroll would enter the screen but not scroll completely off. **(SEE FIGURE 09.)**

Adding Fades and Music

A final render comp was created that dealt with the resizing from the 720x540 Photoshop file to 720x486 for the playback server. This is also where the music and fades were added. This comp is named "pgmguide." I picked a simple name with no spaces or illegal characters in it because it is easier to call it in a script when the name is simple. It is also going to be the name of the file that is rendered from After Effects. The Program Guide 1 comp was nested and fit in the 720x486, 45-second pgmguide comp. I used a 15-frame fade from black and a 15-frame fade to black at the beginning and the end by adding opacity keyframes to the nested comp. I then added a Video Helper (www.videohelper.com) music clip to the render comp and added a 30-frame fade to the end of the music, since I didn't have a version of the music clip that was 45 seconds.**(SEE FIGURE 10.)**

Rendering

The first step to make sure the render would execute correctly is to create a render settings template and an output module template for our playback system and then set them as the default for movies. Once the render settings and output module templates were created and ready, I did a render of the pgmguide comp and saved it to the desktop with the default name that After Effects assigned to the output file, which is pgmguide.mov. One nice thing about After Effects is that once you do a render and pick a location for the output file to be saved to, it remembers that setting and repeats it the next time something is rendered. This is why I needed to do an initial render of the project to make the Desktop the destination for the file. This is important because the AppleScript that moves the file needs to know where to find it. **(SEE FIGURES 11 & 12.)**

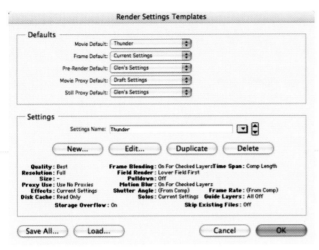

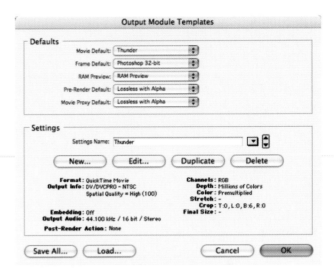

11 & 12 » RENDER SETTINGS AND OUTPUT MODULE SETTINGS

At this point, we have all of the creative elements complete. The Photoshop file and the After Effects project to create the crawl and render them out are ready. Next is building and formatting the text that will be pushed to Photoshop.

Phase 2: Preparing the Programming Data

As I stated before, a FileMaker database is the heart of this system. It is the piece of the puzzle that imports and formats the programming information. It automates the execution of the system, it controls Photoshop and After Effects, and it uploads the final rendered file to the playback server. I chose FileMaker for a few key reasons:

• It can be scheduled to execute tasks.

• It can perform AppleScripts directly from a database.

• It is a fairly easy tool to create a custom solution.

• It is a database, so it can handle and format the programming information.

Not to worry, this is not going to be a lesson on FileMaker, but I do want to explain how the system accounts for the fact that the amount of programming in each day can vary, and the process of making sure that there was enough data to fit within the 45-second scroll. **(SEE FIGURE 13.)**

13 » FILEMAKER PRO LAYOUT THAT CONTROLS THE SYSTEM

For further examination, open the file Program Guide Builder.fp5. The file is unlocked, so if you are familiar with FileMaker, you can examine the scripts and fields to see how it works.

The first challenge was that the names of the programs were in some cases longer than one line of text. The titles needed to wrap from one line to the next based on how long they were. The wrap setting in the database controls this. It counts the number of

Guide Data						26 Shows - 68 Lines
Date To Set:					Wrap	Repeat
3/28/2005		Show Date	Today		40	33
6:00 AM - Traffic Check						

14 » TEXT WRAP SETTING

Guide Data						26 Shows - 68 Lines
Date To Set:					Wrap	Repeat
3/28/2005		Show Date	Today		40	33
6:00 AM - Traffic Check						

15 » REPEATS SCROLL BASED ON LINE COUNT

16 » ADDITIONAL MESSAGES ADDED TO THE END OF A SCROLL

characters and then wraps at a space as close to the wrap number as possible. (SEE FIGURE 14.)

The second challenge was to make the scroll long enough to fill the 45-second time frame. In some cases the amount of programming was enough lines to fill the scroll. In a case where that wasn't the situation, there were a few options. If the number of lines in the program guide were less than the repeat amount, then the entire guide would scroll twice. (SEE FIGURE 15.)

If there were more lines than the repeat amount, then a short, medium, or long message would be added to create enough lines to fill the scroll. These messages could be promos for the stations web site, new programming notes, or any other promotional messages they wanted to add to a given day's program guide. (SEE FIGURE 16.)

This made the length of the content fairly consistent in the number of lines it contained, while the database decided how to format it based on how much data was available.

⚙ SCHEDULING FILEMAKER

By default, FileMaker does not have any built-in capabilities to schedule scripts to run at certain times. This functionality was achieved using the oAzium Events plug-in from Waves in Motion (www.wmotion.com).

Phase 3: Automating the System

The last phase of the project was to automate all of these elements and make them work together. Even though the FileMaker database triggers everything, it is AppleScript that does all of the heavy lifting and makes it all come together. The AppleScript is provided as well so you can dissect it and see how it works. Let's do that together now and look at the process, sequence, and wording to make this work. NOTE: The ActionApp AppleScript is an executable application that runs the process. View the Action-App.txt to see the code. You can also open the ActionApp with Script Editor in the Applications>AppleScript folder on your hard drive.

:: GETTING THE VARIABLES

The first step of the AppleScript is to set internal variables to values from the FileMaker database. These variables include the composition in After Effects that needs to be rendered, the After Effects project that gets opened, the Photoshop file that gets opened, the text that gets set to the date and guide layers in Photoshop, the network disk that the rendered file gets uploaded to, and more. Instead of hard-coding all of this information in the AppleScript, I chose to store them as fields in the database so if files changed, I could change them in my database's interface. (SEE FIGURE 17.)

:: UPDATING THE PHOTOSHOP FILE

The next portion of the script tells the Finder to open the Photoshop file. It then instructs Photoshop to put the date text into the Date layer and the guide text into the Guide layer. To avoid any errors from popping up along the way, I check first to see if there is any text in the dateref and guideref variable, and then also wrap

```
--Retrieve and set all of the variables from FileMaker PRO
tell application "FileMaker Developer"
    set mycomp to cell "AEComp" of current record of database "Program Guide Builder.fp5"
    set myaefile to cell "AEProject" of current record of database "Program Guide Builder.fp5"
    set mypsfile to cell "PSProject" of current record of database "Program Guide Builder.fp5"
    set mypsfilename to cell "PSProjectShort" of current record of database "Program Guide Builder.fp5"
    set dateref to cell "c_Photoshop format date" of current record of database "Program Guide Builder.fp5"
    set guideref to cell "g_Photoshop format text" of current record of database "Program Guide Builder.fp5"
    set sourcefile to cell "SourceFile" of current record of database "Program Guide Builder.fp5"
    set NetDestination to cell "NetDestination" of current record of database "Program Guide Builder.fp5"
end tell
```

17 » APPLESCRIPT THAT PULLS VARIABLES FROM FILEMAKER PRO

```
--Open the Photoshop file, set the text from FileMaker to the layers in Photoshop.
tell application "Finder"
    open mypsfile as alias
end tell
tell application "Adobe Photoshop CS2"
    with timeout of 10000 seconds
        if dateref = "" then
        else
            try
                set contents of text object of layer "Date" of document mypsfilename to dateref
            end try
        end if
        if guideref = "" then
        else
            try
                set contents of text object of layer "Guide" of document mypsfilename to guideref
            end try
        end if
        close the document mypsfilename saving yes
    end timeout
end tell
```

18 » APPLESCRIPT THAT MOVES DATA TO PHOTOSHOP

the command in a try statement which will capture any errors that come back from Photoshop and keep the process from stalling. AppleScript has a default timeout of one minute. Since it takes Photoshop some time to open the file, set the text, and then save the file, I put in a custom timeout of 10,000 seconds to make sure that it had plenty of time to complete its task. (SEE FIGURE 18.)

:: RENDERING THE AFTER EFFECTS PROJECT

The next section first tells the Finder to open the After Effects file defined by the variable from the FileMaker database. Because After Effects does not accept many commands from AppleScript, the control over After Effects has to come as in as JavaScript. The first step is to create the JavaScript that will add my pgmguide comp to the Render Queue. This is set to the variable myscript1. The second JavaScript tells After Effects to render the Render Queue and close the After Effects project file without saving it. The reason that we don't want to save the After Effects file is that we don't want the Render Queue to grow over time. These JavaScript commands are then sent to After Effects, again with a 10,000-second timeout. The long timeout is very important here be-

cause of the render time involved with the project. (SEE FIGURE 19.)

:: MOVING THE RENDERED FILE TO THE PLAYBACK SERVER

The last step of the script is to mount the network drive for the playback server (this is accomplished by opening an alias to the drive called Connect to Server which is located on the desktop), move the rendered file to it, empty the Trash, and delete the file after it is moved. There are a few important issues that can arise at this step.

1. The file named pgmguide.mov (source-file) needs to be moved to the Trash after it is copied to the playback server. If it is not, After Effects will name the next day's file pgmguide-1.mov because one named pgmguide.mov already exists in that location. This will prevent the AppleScript from copying the correct file to the playback server.

2. You need to empty the Trash. If you do not, on an unattended computer you run the risk of eating up your disk space and running out of room to store each day's rendered movie. I chose to empty the Trash before moving the current file to it so that I always have the most recent file locally if I need it.

```
--Open the After Effects project, add the pgmguide comp to the render que, and render the movie.
tell application "Finder"
    open myaefile as alias
end tell
--Add the comp to the render que
set myscript1 to "
{
searchString = \"" & mycomp & "\";

if (searchString)
{
    searchString = searchString.toLowerCase();
    for (i = 1; i <= app.project.numItems; ++i) {
        var curItem = app.project.item(i);

        if (curItem instanceof CompItem) {
            if (curItem.name.toLowerCase().indexOf(searchString) != -1) {
                app.project.renderQueue.items.add(curItem);
            }
        }
        app.project.renderQueue.showWindow(true);
    }
}
}
"

--Start rendering the render que
set myscript2 to "
{
    var myQueue = app.project.renderQueue
    myQueue.render();
    app.project.close(CloseOptions.DO_NOT_SAVE_CHANGES)
}
"

tell application "Adobe After Effects 6.5"
    with timeout of 10000 seconds
        DoScript myscript1
        DoScript myscript2
    end timeout
end tell
```

19 » APPLESCRIPT THAT RENDERS AFTER EFFECTS ANIMATION

```
--Move the redered movie to the playback server and then delete it from the local machine.
tell application "Finder"
    with timeout of 10000 seconds
        open file "Connect to Server"
        delay 10
        close window "pgmguide"
        move the file sourcefile to the folder NetDestination with replacing
        delay 10
        empty trash
        delete the file sourcefile
    end timeout
end tell
```

20 » APPLESCRIPT THAT MOVES FINAL RENDER AND DELETES IT LOCALLY

Again, I used a long timeout setting because the network copy typically takes longer than one minute. **(SEE FIGURE 20.)**

Once the design and automation work was completed, the files were put on an old iMac we had in storage. It is a fairly slow machine, but since all it does is build these animations in the middle of the night, it was enough to get the job done without spending any extra money. Aside from making sure it was networked and setting the power-saving settings to keep the machine from going to sleep, it was a very basic setup. After Effects, Photoshop, and FileMaker were all that were necessary on this machine. It has been successfully building program guides for over a year now without ever being restarted. Every night at 1 A.M. the system builds a new animation for the day, and our viewers have up-to-date information on our programming without any human effort at all.

ABOUT THE AUTHOR

Glen Stephens has been involved in the television production industry for over 15 years and has a Bachelor's Degree in Television Production from Arizona State University. He is currently the Station Manager for Mesa Channel 11, an Adjunct Faculty Member at Arizona State University teaching Television Production Techniques and Advanced Multimedia Production for the Walter Cronkite School of Journalism and Telecommunications.

Glen owns Pixel Post Studios, LLC, a commercial software and consulting company that specializes in software development for broadcast-related graphic development, and he is a contributing writer to Photoshop User magazine. Glen is the creator of the Tools for Television Photoshop Toolbox, as well as Tools for Television PRO, an add-on utility that adds broadcast features to Photoshop (www.toolsfortelevision.com). Glen has also contributed to and co-authored books on broadcast graphics, including Photoshop for Nonlinear Editors, Broadcast Graphics On the Spot, and Teach Yourself Adobe Premiere in 24 Hours.

Resources

www.php.net

AppleScript in a Nutshell
Bruce W. Perry (O'Reilly 2001)

www.filemaker.com

www.wmotion.com

www.apple.com/macosx/features/applescript/

www.filemakermagazine.com

www.macscripter.net

Creating Motion Graphics with After Effects, Volumes 1 and 2
Trish and Chris Meyer (CMP Books 2004/2005)

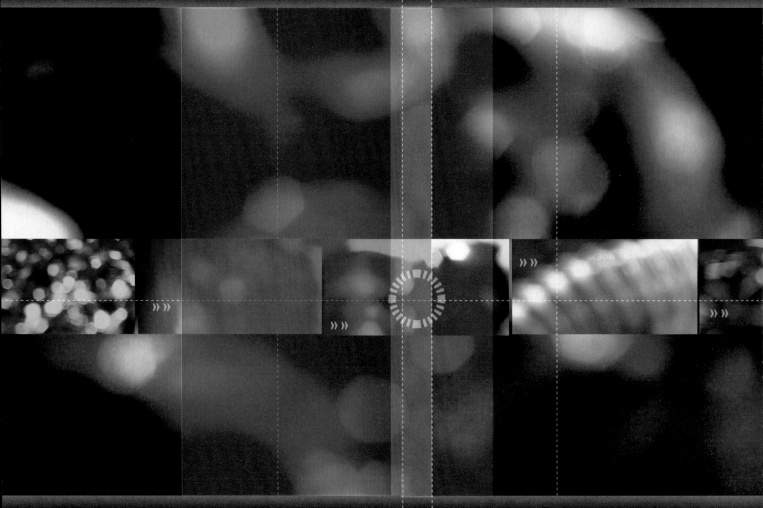

DVD MENUS, START TO FINISH:
HOW TO BUILD A DVD MENU

RICHARD HARRINGTON, RHED PIXEL

I've been meaning to teach this lesson for a long time. The teacher in me is excited to share this technique. The business owner was a little hesitant to let you in on one of my company's greatest secrets. Let me start off by saying a few things:

• These techniques are not difficult.

• The equipment needed is very modest.

• You have to learn to trust yourself.

• The render times are very short.

• This really does work.

• Your clients will be impressed.

"Okay," you say... why so much justification? Well, I've got a very useful secret. Making your own looping backgrounds and DVD menus is not very hard. In fact, you can use random objects and "bad" videography to pull it off. We have a motion graphics shoot every other month in my office, and it has come to be known as "Shiny Stuff Day."

WHAT'S ON THE DVD
Sample Footage Plates, After Effects Projects, and Sample Render Backgrounds

01 »

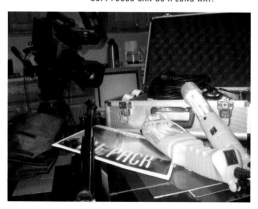

02 » A LITTLE BIT OF CREATIVE LIGHTING AND SOFT FOCUS CAN GO A LONG WAY.

03 » THE GEAR NEEDED IS PRETTY SIMPLE. WHILE WE USED A MIDRANGE CAMERA, ANY DV CAMERA WILL DO. HOWEVER, A TRIPOD IS A MUST.

Getting Started

These techniques involve just a little bit of optical "squinting." By playing with your camera and subject, you can easily achieve great looks within the camera. The goal is to not finish the job in the camera, but great footage goes along way towards great graphics. Trust yourself here. As long as you are willing to experiment, you can achieve great creative results. Creativity involves the ability to let go of your fear and take chances. **(SEE FIGURE 01 & 02.)**

Technical Approach

In my experiences as a trainer and speaker, I have found that less than 20% of my audiences use blending (or transfer) modes. This is a crime that I intend to fix. By employing simple footage, blending modes, and some optical trickery, beautiful backgrounds can be made. **(SEE FIGURE 03.)**

Stages

1. Gathering objects to shoot
   15 minutes to 4 hours (depending on your ambition)

2. Shooting and lighting objects:
   1–4 hours

3. Creating the background:
   10–30 minutes after practice (this includes render time)

✱ SHINY STUFF EXAMPLES

- :: Wrapped mints
- :: Metal candle holders
- :: Plastic boxes
- :: Light disc
- :: Award statues
- :: Kitchen utensils

- :: Jewelry pieces
- :: Crystal glass
- :: Liquids of various densities
- :: Holiday lights
- :: Scientific flasks
- :: Dinner plates

- :: Porcelain fixtures
- :: Metal air vents
- :: Electric fans
- :: Candles

Budget

If you already own production gear, you can pull this together with as little as $35 for a shoplight and some gels. We usually budget $100 per shoot.

Get It Together

It's important to find interesting objects to shoot. Anything that reflects light is an awesome candidate. Colorful objects produce nice results. Highly reflective surfaces like porcelain and metal can be very useful. Knick-knacks and drawer contents can work. Just tell your team to bring things in to shoot. You'll be surprised by the diversity of objects they'll bring and even more surprised by the results you'll get. **(SEE FIGURE 04.)**

Make It Happen

Any video camera will work, but try to shoot in a digital format that will allow you to cleanly transfer the files to your system. Some flaws of video like flares and hotspots will actually come in handy. If you have access to camera filters, a soft FX filter or Pro Mist filter can help soften your image. Before shooting, ensure that your lens is clean. Extra dust or smudges on the lens won't help you here. More useful than the camera will be your tripod. The movement in the textures will usually come from moving the lights or objects, not the camera. This is where the field monitor will come in handy. By being able to see your results, you can make variations in the speed and type of movement. Your best results will often come from macro shots, or extreme close-ups. Camera movement will be too jarring when tightly focused. **(SEE FIGURE 05.)**

04 »

compact disc

porcellain tile

computer keyboard

05 »

06 » THESE HANDHELD SHOPLIGHTS ARE INEXPENSIVE AND PRODUCE BRIGHT HIGHLIGHTS. PLUS, THEY REMAIN COOL TO THE TOUCH AND ARE A SAFER OPTION.

07 » A FIELD MONITOR AND LIGHTING GELS ARE IMPORTANT PIECES FOR THIS PRODUCTION. EXTRA LIGHTS CAN BE USED AS WELL TO PROVIDE SOFT LIGHTINNG.

Light the Way

You're about to spend some time in the dark. Be sure your shooting environment is set up with what you need and that your props are handy. You will also want the ability to easily turn lights off and on in the room to make setups easier. While a few studio lights can be useful, you can also get away with cheaper shoplights from a hardware store. The most useful item for lighting is handheld shoplights. These small fluorescent lights can put off enough light for your project. They are also cool to the touch and lightweight. This will allow you to create subtle motion as the light moves across the surface of the images. The use of gentle rhythmic movement will give you the needed sense of motion for your motion graphics. While you can always add color effects to your After Effects comp, don't be afraid to try another type of filter. Lighting gels can be easily bought from professional lighting stores, at audio centers that cater to DJs, or from online vendors. We keep a "party pack" with our lights that contains several different colors. You can tape the gels around your handheld lights (or even in front of the camera lens) to add important color. **(SEE FIGURE 06-09.)**

And Action!

It's now time to shoot. When you start your cameras rolling, be sure to get enough footage. I recommend that you roll for 1–3 minutes on each shot. This will give you plenty of variation to

08 » THE KEY IS TO MOVE THE LIGHTS, NOT THE CAMERA.

09 » SMALL MOVEMENT PRODUCES THE BEST RESULTS.

choose from and more than enough footage to make longer loop-ing backgrounds. Remember to experiment with focus and iris. Don't be afraid to try out an idea here. Just watch your confidence monitor to make sure things are working. Keep an eye on your white level to ensure the video is not getting too hot. These types of shots are prone to overexposure. While you're shooting, also consider capturing some still photos for use in high-resolution print projects.

Once you trigger the camera, it is okay to step away (provided it's on a secure tripod). The goal is to minimize any movement of the camera. Take advantage of your turntable or lazy susan. Even without rotating the object, the subtle motion of moving the handheld lights will give you great results.

The goal is to create as much magic within the camera as pos-sible. But don't worry—After Effects is only going to make things better in the end. **(SEE FIGURE 10–12.)**

Load It Up

At some point, you'll stop shooting (it's okay to be a little sad... but you can come back again). You'll need to move back to the post-production side and get the footage into your computer. You don't really need a full-blown editing application, just some way to load your footage in. Both Macs and PCs have free solutions available for capturing digital video over FireWire. Here's some tips to ensure your success.

- Be sure to clearly label the clips with a descriptive name.
- Capture in the highest-quality mode you can.
- To get the most mileage from your footage, you should con-sider investing in an external drive to hold it. This way it can be easily shared with others in your office.
- If your editing system does not capture to a format that After Effects can read, you'll likely want to create subclips and re-export the footage to your drive.
- Be sure your clips have proper file extensions. It is common for editing programs to not add the needed tags.

10 » WE HAD THE LIGHTS ON FOR THE PHOTO. IF YOU AREN'T AFRAID, SHOOT IN THE DARK.

11 » FASTEN THE LIGHTING GELS WITH SCOTCH TAPE FOR EASY REMOVAL.

12 » THE FIELD MONITOR IS THE BEST WAY TO SEE YOUR RESULTS. THIS WILL ENSURE THAT YOU WON'T TOUCH THE CAMERA AND GET JITTERY MOTION.

13 » BEAD STORES FOR JEWELRY MAKING ARE A GOOD PLACE TO START, AS ARE AUTOMO-TIVE, HARDWARE, OR OFFICE SUPPLY STORES.

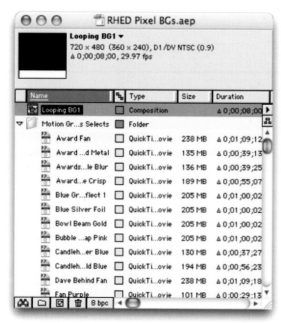

14 » HOLD DOWN THE OPTION/ALT KEY TO DRAG AN ENTIRE LENGTH OF
FOOTAGE INTO YOUR PROJECT.

15 » TIME STRETCH
YOUR FOOTAGE TO
PRODUCE SLOWER
MOVEMENT IN THE
BACKGROUND, IF
NEEDED. BE SURE
TO TRY FRAME
BLENDING WITH
MOTION EFFECTS
APPLIED.

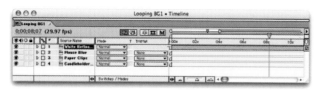

16 » RANDOMLY TRY THREE TO FOUR FOOTAGE CLIPS IN YOUR TIMELINE. TO GET
YOU STARTED, I'VE INCLUDED SOME SAMPLE FOOTAGE.

Start Your Engines

It's now time to switch over to After Effects. If you don't have
access to After Effects, you can pull these same techniques off
using Discreet Combustion or Apple Motion. The key here is you
need a Timeline-based motion graphics application that can support blending (transfer) modes. The ability to nest or precompose
will also come in handy.

Blending modes are an incredibly powerful feature of compositing
applications that determine how one layer interacts with another.
Elements can interact in new and exciting ways thanks to blending modes. The easiest way to learn blending modes is to just try
them. To cycle through them in Adobe applications, hold down
the Shift key and press either the minus key or the plus key.

Filters take on new life when you blend a filtered copy of a layer
over the original. Blending modes can also solve the problem
of knocking out a white or black background. My favorite use
of blending modes is creating moving backgrounds for use in a
video project. Let's take some of the great footage made earlier in
this tutorial and put it to work.

Import and Build

1. Create a new project. Save and name the file.

2. It's time to bring your captured clips into After Effects. You can
    choose File>Import or drag them into the project window.

3. Select three to five clips that you'd like to use and drag them on
    the new composition icon. This will create a new comp with all
    your footage layers.

4. Check your composition settings by pressing Cmd+K (Ctrl+K).
    From the preset menu, choose NTSC DV, 720X480, and gave the
    comp a better name. Also, set the duration to 30:00

5. If your footage is not long enough, you can stretch it by choos-
    ing Layer>Time Stretch. Go with even increments like 200%
    when stretching a layer. Enable frame blending as well for all
    stretched layers. (SEE FIGURE 14–16.)

Mix and Blend

1. Turn off all layers except the bottommost two. Adjust the blending modes on the top layer until you find a look that you like. Experiment with blur filters on the top layer and adjust opacity to personal taste.

2. Click RAM Preview to see your results.

3. Repeat the blending technique on the remaining layers.

4. Try changing the stacking order and opacity to achieve additional options.

5. Click RAM Preview or press 0 on the numeric keypad to see your results.

6. To create the soft bloom, add an Adjustment Layer. Apply the Gaussian Blur effect and adjust the layer's blending mode and opacity settings.

7. Solo your bottommost layer for easy viewing. For greater visual impact, I recommend boosting the intensity of your bottom layer. You can do this through a Levels adjustment. (SEE FIGURE 17.)

Make the Loop

1. Now it's time to create the loop. Highlight all of your footage layers. Create a precomposition by choosing Layer>Precompose or pressing Shift+Cmd+C (Shift+Ctrl+C). Name the precomp footage BG.

2. Access your composition settings by pressing Shift+Cmd+K (Shift+Ctrl+K) and shorten the comp to be 25:00.

3. Go to the 12:00 mark by pressing Cmd+G (Ctrl+G) and entering 12:00.

4. Split the layer which will create the loop point. Select the layer and press Shift+Cmd+D (Shift+Ctrl+D).

5. We now must overlap the layers. With Layer 1 active, jump to the end of the composition by pressing the End key on your keyboard. Press the right bracket key (]) to move the layer's outpoint.

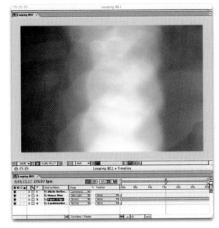

17 » DIFFERENT MODES EQUAL DIFFERENT RESULTS. BE SURE TO EXPERIMENT.

18 » IT IS NECESSARY TO PRECOM-
POSE YOUR TIMELINE IN ORDER
TO CREATE THE LOOP.

19 » TO MOVE AROUND QUICKLY,
PRESS CMD+G/CTRL+G TO CALL
UP THE GO TO TIME DIALOG BOX.

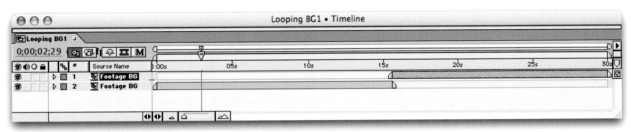

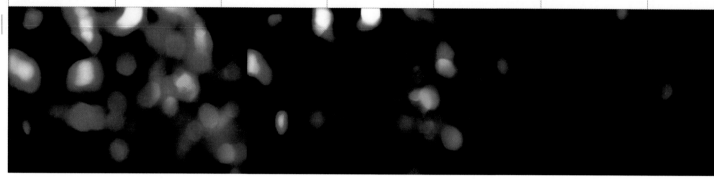

6. Select Layer 2 then press the Home key. Press the left bracket key ([) to move the layer's in-point.

7. Activate Layer 1 and press I to jump to the layer's in-point.

8. Press Option+T (Alt+T) for opacity and activate the stopwatch.

9. Set a keyframe to 0% opacity.

10. Jump forward four-and-a-half seconds by pressing Cmd+G, then typing +4:15.

11. Set a keyframe to 100% opacity.

12. Flip the quality switches to Best Quality. (SEE FIGURE 18-22.)

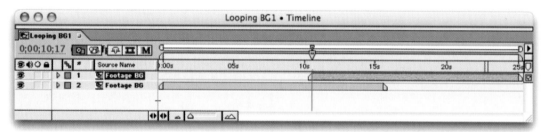

21 » A FEW SECONDS OVERLAP IS
IMPORTANT FOR THE LOOP.

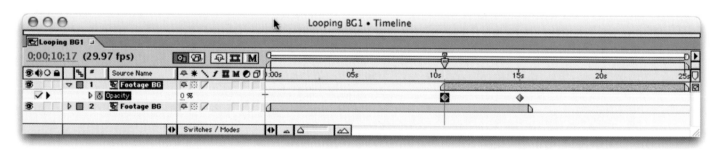

22 » THE PASCUZZI RULE: IF YOU CAN'T
SOLVE IT... DISSOLVE IT. SAGE ADVICE.

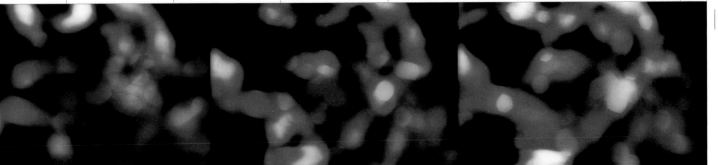

Color Your Background

1. By placing an Adjustment Layer on top, you can apply global effects or adjustments to all layers below. Use this to tweak your saturation or intensity. Add an Adjustment Layer at the top of your stack (Layer> New> Adjustment Layer).

2. Apply a colorization effect such as Colorama (Effect>Image Control> Colorama), Tint (Effect> Image Control>Tint) or Hue/Saturation with the colorize option selected (Effect>Adjust>Hue/Saturation).

3. You may want to apply the Effect>Video>Broadcast Colors filter. Other filters can be applied for a global effect as well. It is significantly faster to apply an Adjustment Layer, then to render individual effects on each layer.

4. You may also experiment with other effects on the Adjustment Layer such as Glow, Blur, Light Burst or Trapcode's Shine.

5. Make sure frame blending is enabled and check your layer blending modes. Flip all your quality switches to Best, and render at Lossless Settings. (SEE FIGURE 23.)

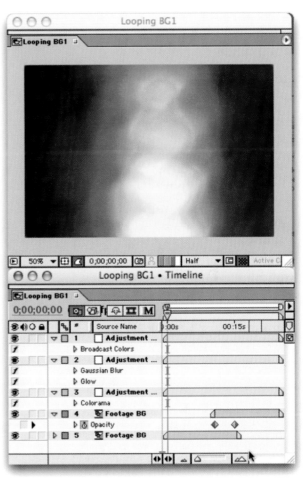

23 » GRAY BACKGROUNDS ARE BORING...
A LITTLE BIT OF COLORAMA CAN GO A LONG WAY.

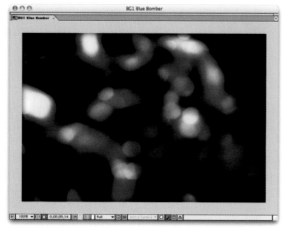

24 »

🖐 🔊 ○ 🔒		🖐 #	Source Name	Mode	T	TrkMat
👁		▷ ☐ 1	Glitter Mints.mov	Soft Light ▼		
👁		▷ ☐ 2	Globs.mov	Hue ▼		None
👁		▷ ☐ 3	Metal.mov	Overlay ▼		None
👁		▷ ☐ 4	Reflect Gold.mov	Normal ▼		None

25 » WHILE THIS RECIPE PRODUCES THE BACKGROUND ABOVE, YOU SHOULD FEEL
FREE TO TRY NEW COMBINATIONS.

Sample Recipes to Try

To make this concept come to life, I've included some source footage on the DVD-ROM. You can use the following recipes to practice and get the technique down.

Blue Bomber Background

1. **Import the following movies into your project:**

    :: **Glitter Mints.mov**
    :: **Globs.mov**
    :: **Metal.mov**
    :: **Reflect Gold.mov**

2. **Create a new composition with the NTSC DV 720X480 preset and set the duration to 20 seconds.**

3. **Arrange the clips as follows and set their blending mode as follows:**

    Track 1: Glitter Mints.mov, Mode Soft Light
    Track 2: Globs.mov, Mode Hue
    Track 3: Metal.mov, Mode Overlay
    Track 4: Reflect Gold.mov, Mode Normal

4. **Precompose the four tracks and perform the previously mentioned looping technique.**

    :: **Select all four layers and press Shift+Cmd+C (Shift+Ctrl+C). Name the precomp Blue Nest.**
    :: **Shorten your working comp to 15 seconds by pressing Cmd+K (Ctrl+K) and modifying the duration.**
    :: **Go to the 10-second mark by pressing Cmd+G (Ctrl+G) and entering 10:00.**
    :: **Press Shift+Cmd+D (Shift+Ctrl+D) to split the layer.**
    :: **Relocate the two layers in the Timeline. Set Layer 1's in-point to 00:00. Set Layer 2's out-point to 14:29.**
    :: **Keyframe an Opacity Transition from 100% to 0% on Layer 1 where the two layers overlap.**
    :: **You now have a loop! Launch a RAM Preview to check.**

5. **Add an Adjustment Layer by choosing Layer>New Adjustment Layer.**

6. Apply a Gaussian Blur effect and set the radius to 20 pixels.

7. Set the Adjustment Layer's blending mode to Overlay.

8. Render or further modify. **(SEE FIGURE 24 & 25.)**

RHED Gold Background

1. Import the following movies into your project:

   :: **Glitter Mints.mov**
   :: **Gold to Blue.mov**
   :: **Paper Clips.mov**
   :: **Soda 1.mov**

2. Create a new composition with the NTSC DV 720X480 preset and set the duration to 20 seconds.

3. Arrange the clips as follows and set their blending modes as follows:

   Track 1: Gold to Blue.mov, Mode Hard Light
   Track 2: Soda 1.mov, Mode Lighten
   Track 3: Paper Clips.mov, Mode Overlay
   Track 4: Glitter Mints.mov, Mode Normal

4. Add an Adjustment Layer as Layer 3. Apply a Gaussian Blur effect with a radius of 15 pixels.

5. Precompose the four tracks and perform the previously mentioned looping technique.

6. Create a new comp-sized solid layer by pressing Cmd+Y (Ctrl+Y). Set the color to R:200 G:50 B:20. Change the solid's blending mode to Color.

7. Add an Adjustment Layer by choosing Layer>New Adjustment Layer.

8. Apply a Gaussian Blur effect and set the radius to 10 pixels.

9. Set the adjustment layer's blending mode to Screen.

10. Render or further modify. **(SEE FIGURE 26-27.)**

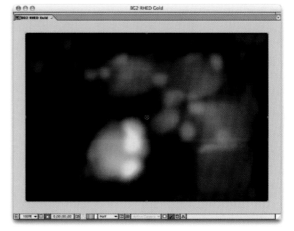

26 »

27 » AN ADJUSTMENT LAYER WAS USED TO FURTHER SOFTEN THE FOOTAGE. YOU CAN ALSO TRY CHANGING AN ADJUSTMENT LAYER'S MODE FOR NEW LOOKS.

28 »

Mike's Moxie Background

1. Import the following movies into your project:

   :: Blue Hexes.mov
   :: Green Soda.mov
   :: Organic.mov
   :: Metal.mov

2. Create a new composition with the NTSC DV 720X480 preset and set the duration to 20 seconds.

3. Arrange the clips as follows and set their Blending Mode

   Track 1: Green Soda.mov, Mode Overlay
   Track 2: Blue Hexes.mov, Mode Soft Light
   Track 3: Metal.mov, Mode Add
   Track 4: Organic.mov, Mode Normal

4. Precompose the four tracks and perform the previously mentioned looping technique.

5. Add an Adjustment Layer by choosing Layer>New Adjustment Layer. Apply a Gaussian Blur effect set to a radius of 20 pixels.

6. Add an Adjustment Layer by choosing Layer>New Adjustment Layer. Apply the Colorama effect. Set the Output Cycle to Solarize Green.

7. Set the Colorama Adjustment Layer's blending mode to Hue.

8. Render or further modify. (SEE FIGURE 28–31.)

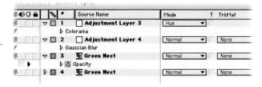

29 »

30 » COLORAMA HAS THE WORST DEFAULT PRESET OF ANY FILTER. DON'T BE TURNED OFF... INSTEAD OPEN UP THE OUTPUT CYCLE AREA AND EXPERIMENT.

31 » BY SETTING THE COLORAMA ADJUSTMENT LAYER'S MODE TO HUE, A MORE SUBTLE COLOR EFFECT WAS ACHIEVED.

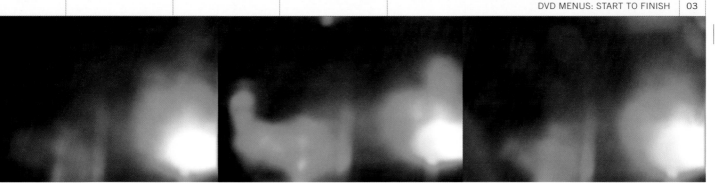

Do It Your Way

At this point, you need to finish the menu. You may choose to utilize your full toolbox here. Perhaps you'll just take your looping background into a DVD authoring application such Adobe Encore or Apple DVD Studio Pro. You can also take advantage of the powerful compositing and masking abilities of After Effects.

The point is to build your menu until you (or your client) is happy. If you finish in After Effects, you'll need to create a highlight layer for your rollover effects. (**SEE FIGURE 32.**)

Export Highlight Layer

Your DVD authoring app is going to need a map image to determine what lights up. This grayscale image identifies where the glows appear. It is an overlay for the moving video file.

1. **Complete your DVD menu and render out the final version using a lossless codec.**

2. **Save your After Effects file to capture any changes.**

3. **Set your Comp window to 100% and Full Quality.**

4. **Go to a representative frame and choose Composition>Save Frame As>Photoshop Layers.**

5. **Open the file in Photoshop to further modify it. If you open it in Photoshop CS, check that the Pixel Aspect Ratio settings are flagged as non-square.**

6. **Turn off the visibility icon (eyeball) for all layers that are not part of the highlight layer.**

7. **Select one of the visible layers and choose Merge Visible from the Layers palette submenu.**

8. **Lock the transparency for this new merged layer by checking the Lock Transparent Pixels box.**

9. **Choose Edit>Fill and fill with black (or white, depending on your DVD application). (SEE FIGURE 33.)**

32 »

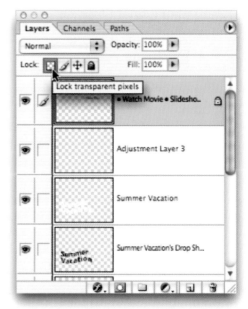

33 » BY USING LOCK TRANSPORT PIXELS, IT IS MUCH EASIER TO GET A CLEAN FILL ON THE HIGHLIGHT LAYER.

:: Square vs. Non-Square Pixel Aspect Ratio

DVDs use non-square pixels. If you are building in Photoshop CS or After Effects, this is no problem.

:: The Screen Is Smaller Than You Think

All words must fall within the title-safe area, which is 80% of the screen. All logos or elements meant to be seen in their entirety must fall inside of the action-safe area, which is 90% of the screen.

:: Final File Ends Up 720X480 Pixels for NTSC

Whether its widescreen or standard, you still have an area that's only 720 pixels across and 480 pixels tall to design for.

:: Start High ... Finish Low

Design your DVD elements at the highest-quality codec available to you. It's better to give your compression program a high-quality file. Even if you are using footage acquired from a DVD, render out to the Animation (or another lossless) codec before going to MPEG-2.

34 » AN AE COMP CAN BE SAVED OUT AS A LAYERED PSD FILE. THIS IS AN IMPORTANT STEP IF YOU NEED TO MAKE A HIGHLIGHT LAYER FOR YOUR MOTION BACKGROUND.

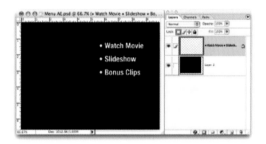

35 » DIFFERENT DVD APPS REQUIRE DIFFERENT HIGHLIGHT LAYERS. YOURS MAY WANT A WHITE ON BLACK IMAGE OR THE INVERSE. BE SURE TO READ UP.

10. Create a new empty layer and place it in the background.

11. Select All, then fill this layer with white (or black, again depending on your DVD application). The goal is to create a high-contrast matte.

12. Delete any unused layers from your Photoshop document.

13. Choose File>Save As to and save a flattened PICT or TARGA file.

14. Save the layered Photoshop file so you can make future modifications.

15. Duplicate the flattened file, open it, and choose Select All. Pressing Cmd+I (Ctrl+I) to Invert the image. This way you'll have both for your DVD authoring application if needed. (SEE FIGURE 34-35.)

Real World Setup

Where does the motion graphic artist fit into the DVD process? As the menu designer of course! While many people settle for built-in templates or stock backgrounds, that often won't cut it. Making your own custom backgrounds is essential as you build your reputation and client base.

While you may be turned off by the time involved in shooting, don't be. In a very short amount of time you can build an immense library of footage. This raw material can be used not only for DVD backgrounds but also for animated backgrounds, bumpers, lower-third bars, and more. Take the leap and grab your camera (but in the meantime I've included 10 clips to get you started).

ABOUT THE AUTHOR

Richard Harrington is a certified Project Management Professional, Apple Certified Trainer in Final Cut Pro, and Adobe Certified Expert in Photoshop and After Effects. Additionally, he has completed Avid's Master Editor Workshop and the Avid Certified Instructor Program. His visual communications consultancy, RHED Pixel, creates motion graphics and produces video and multimedia projects, specializing in producing content or non-profit associations and live events. More information is available at www.RHEDPixel.com. He is a faculty member at The Art Institute of Washington, a popular speaker at conferences, and an instructor for Future Media Concepts.

Richard is the author of *Photoshop CS for Nonlinear Editors* and co-author of *Final Cut Pro On the Spot* and *After Effects On the Spot*. If you have more Photoshop questions, Richard can be reached as moderator of Creative Cow's Photoshop Forum.

Special thanks to the RHED Pixel Crew: Mark Weiser, Sara Evans, Dennis Byrne, Dave Phillips, Mark Hofmann, and Meghan Ryan-Harrington.

RECOMMENDED RESOURCES

Okay, I believe in my own work. These are good books (in my opinion, of course).

Photoshop CS for Nonlinear Editors

Final Cut Pro On the Spot

After Effects On the Spot

Photoshop Dream Team Volume One

Photoshop CS: Essentials for Digital Video (DVD) from www.vasst.com

Photoshop CS2 Killer Tips

DVD Demystified

Designing Menus with Encore DVD

Broadcast Graphics On the Spot

ANIMATION WITH FLASH AND AFTER EFFECTS

DAVE E. PHILLIPS

Have you seen what the kids are watching these days? Look familiar? It should because there's a good chance the software used is the same application that created the e-card you sent your mum on her birthday: Macromedia Flash. Flash has made the opportunity of producing quality animation accessible to almost anyone. To take animation to the next level, however, you'll need a tool designed to add visual splendor and make it ready for broadcast. Enter Adobe After Effects.

In this chapter you'll learn how to combine the best qualities of both applications to get your animation ready for broadcast. I'll assume that you've had previous experience in 2D animation and that you have an intermediate understanding of Flash. So, without further delay, get your Wacom warmed up.

WHAT'S ON THE DVD

Included on the DVD are all the source files for the project and a completed rendered sequence. With the supplied resources, you can begin this tutorial at any point simply by using the assets provided.

INTRODUCTION

Parameters

:: THE CHASE

In this chapter you'll be creating a six-shot sequence in which a small purple monkey, Lucid, is being pursued by a giant crab-like monster named Creaton. You'll use Flash to pre-visualize, animate, ink, and color the frame-by-frame animated elements. Then, in Adobe After Effects, you'll pull it together with backgrounds, camera moves, and special effects. Additionally, you'll learn unique techniques such as how to create a "2½D" looping background cycle and how to make "Walt quality" shadows.

:: TOOLS NEEDED:

- Macromedia Flash MX 2004 or later.
- An image-editing application such as Adobe Photoshop
- Either a digital tablet or a scanner (for importing hand-drawn artwork)
- An inhuman amount of patience

:: ESTIMATED HOURS

(However the finished Flash files are provided if you want to skip forward several steps)

- Storyboards and animatic: 5 hours
- Rough animation, ink and paint: 40–60 hours
- Digitally painted backgrounds: 12–15 hours
- Special effects and editing: 8 hours
- Musical score: 15 hours

THE SHOT LIST

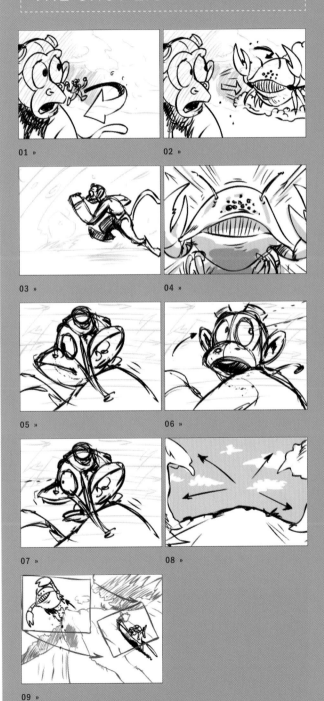

:: **THE PLAN**

Now that you know the premise, here's the shot list:

Shot 1a: Lucid, our primate protagonist, dashes into a clearing in a surreal jungle. **(SEE FIGURE 01.)**

Shot 1b: Just as Lucid breathes a sigh of relief, Creaton explodes into the scene and the chase begins. **(SEE FIGURE 02.)**

Shot 2: Lucid runs though the jungle. **(SEE FIGURE 03.)**

Shot 3: Creaton gallops close behind. **(SEE FIGURE 04.)**

Shot 4a: Lucid running. **(SEE FIGURE 05.)**

Shot 4b: Lucid looks behind at Creaton. **(SEE FIGURE 06.)**

Shot 4c: A shocked Lucid turns to see the approaching cliff. **(SEE FIGURE 07.)**

Shot 5: The approaching precipice! **(SEE FIGURE 08.)**

Shot 6: Lucid skids to the edge of the cliff and narrowly keeps from going over. He looks back at Creaton, then turns back and leaps over the left edge. Creaton charges forward, skids over the edge, clings to the cliff for a moment then falls to his doom. The camera booms and tracks to the side of the cliff, where Lucid is safely hanging on a convenient branch. **(SEE FIGURE 09.)**

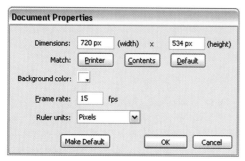

10 » THE DOCUMENT SETTING FOR DV

⚙ ACTION-SAFE AND TITLE-SAFE GUIDES IN FLASH

Creating these guides will keep you aware of what your audience will be seeing on their television sets.

1. On a new layer, create a box the size of your document and delete the fill.

2. Change the stroke color to red.

3. Make two duplicates. Scale the first to 90% of your document and the second to 80%.

4. Select all the boxes and convert it to a symbol and turn the layer into a guide layer.

Tutorial

:: GETTING STARTED IN FLASH

In order to have an animation that can go to video, you'll need to properly set it up in Flash. Head to the Document Properties dialogue (Modify>Document). Since Flash doesn't support non-square pixels, set the Dimensions to 720X534 for final output to NTSC DV (or 720X540 for output to NTSC D1). Then set the Frame Rate to 15 or 30fps. The important thing is that you use a frame rate that After Effects can smoothly translate for video. Most animation for television shoots in twos or more, so every drawing is shown on screen for at least two frames. Choose 15fps and you deal with half the frames in Flash (and half the mess). After Effects then merely needs to double it to output for video. **(SEE FIGURE 10.)**

:: STORYBOARD AND ANIMATICS IN FLASH

Flash's unique toolset makes it an ideal choice for creating pre-visualization. By creating your storyboards in Flash, you can proceed to the animatic without wasting time scanning and breaking up elements. Here are a few tips on the process:

Use a separate scene for each shot.

Create background and characters on separate layers.

Do only enough detail to communicate the shot effectively.

TIP // **PRINTING THE STORYBOARDS** :: To print your boards, select File>Export>Export Movie. Then in the "Save as type" drop-down menu select JPEG Sequence. Then import each file into your favorite graphic application to lay them out to print.

TIP // **TIMING IS EVERYTHING** :: In animation, timing is key. In order to get it right, refine your animatic as much as possible before moving on to rough animation. Remember, it's much easier to re-tween a symbol, than it is to redraw animation.

Create symbols of your characters and Motion Tween them for the animatic.

Keeping elements on separate layers in Flash makes animatics a breeze. **(SEE FIGURE 11.)**

11 »

:: BACKGROUNDS

Backgrounds are a huge factor in making your animation look professional. Traditionally, backgrounds are richly painted. I created these backgrounds in Corel Painter. This method looks great but adds three to five hours per background. So consider your budget when deciding how to render your backgrounds. You may find that Flash works best for your look and budget. Whatever you decide, keep a few things in mind:

Detail of the scenery for Shot 2 **(SEE FIGURE 12.)**

Keep your sketches clean and light, and use them to animate over.

Add a 100-pixel border to your images so you can reframe the shot slightly if needed later. For shots with a stationary camera, such as Shot 1, this means your image size will be 920X734 square pixels.

Pay attention to the title-safe and action-safe areas.

An example of a good background. **(SEE FIGURE 13.)**

12 »

13 »

TIP // **THE PENNY DROPPED** :: Don't know a key from an extreme? Check out *The Animator's Survival Kit* by Richard Williams. I consider this modestly priced book more valuable than the education I'll be paying off until I die. It's a sacred text that no animator should be without.

Paint what the camera sees. Plan your camera moves ahead of time and save yourself from hours of painting areas the audience will never see. **(SEE FIGURE 14.)**

Look at all that used space! Why paint it?

When in doubt, go larger. You don't want to spend time creating backgrounds, only to find out in After Effects that you underestimated.

:: PLANNING MULTI-PLANE EFFECTS

This process involves breaking up the elements of your background into multiple layers or planes for the foreground, middle ground, and background. It's the digital child of the multi-plane camera developed by Disney in the golden age of 2D. When deciding whether to implement this technique, ask these questions:

Will the camera move in the shot?

Do I have scenery in the immediate foreground?

Do the characters move behind parts of the scenery?

Am I using a rack focus effect?

If you answered yes to any of these, then you'll need to set up your scenery accordingly. Group your scenery in layers such as foreground, middle ground and background.

Splitting this scenery along red line will make compositing them with animation headache-free. **(SEE FIGURE 15.)**

:: ANIMATING WITH EASE

Although I won't be teaching you how to animate frame by frame in this chapter, I have compiled some tips designed to help you focus on your animating and streamline the process.

:: ROUGH ANIMATION

First open your animatic FLA file and save it as a new file. Turn your animatic layers into Guide layers and toggle the visibility to reference them while animating. Place your refined background sketch on a layer below and lock it. Use a medium gray for drawing your rough animation so you can see your lines clearly later when you ink it.

Gray lines work best for rough animation. **(SEE FIGURE 16.)**

:: DIGITAL INK AND PAINT

Once you've completed the rough animation and you're happy with it, it's time to ink it. Ink and color your animation on a separate layer above your rough anima-

16 »

tion. Create a separate layer for each element. In the case of Shot 1, create a separate layer for Lucid, Creaton, and Creaton's dust cloud. This separation is vital for implementing effects such as shadows, dust, and rack focus.

:: PAINTING

I find I do more work filling areas that the Close Gaps misses due to the gap threshold than it saves me by closing my gaps. So for coloring, alternate between the Bucket Fill tool (K) set to Don't Close Gaps and the Brush tool (B) set to Paint Behind mode. Choose a color and fill the appropriate areas in the frame. When you run across a shape with a gap that prevents you from filling it, switch to the Brush and dab the gap to close it off. Then go back to the Bucket to fill it. Got tiny areas that are difficult to click to fill? Dab it with the Brush tool. (SEE FIGURE 17.)

A completed frame. (SEE FIGURE 18.)

:: SHADOWS AND HIGHLIGHTS DONE RIGHT

Animators love shortcuts. Who doesn't? In my opinion, however, you should never cut corners on shadows. Using simple techniques, I'll show you how to create beautiful shadows and highlights. Open Shot 1 in Flash; I'll be using it as the example.

:: SHADE OUTSIDE THE LINES

When creating the shadows in Flash, create a separate layer for each character shadow and one for cast shadows. Use the Brush tool with a black fill and the alpha at 60% and draw the shadows for each frame. Later you'll blur them, so shade beyond the lines of the drawings so there won't be a faded edge after applying blur. For Creaton's highlight, on a separate layer add small white dots in the eyes where the light source directly hits. When you finish the highlights in After Effects,

17 » INKING THE ANIMATION.

18 »

⚙ BRUSH SIZE

This is the biggest "gotcha" for the Brush tool. The brush size in Flash is relative to the screen, not the stage. This means that if you draw a stroke zoomed at 100% and then again at 25%, the stroke you drew at 25% will be thicker than the stroke drawn at 100%. This can be a huge hassle for animators, especially when working with multiple animators. So what's the solution? Agree on zoom levels ahead of time. Pick a zoom level for main lines and another for detail lines and then stick with it.

19 » ALL THESE STROKES WHERE CREATED USING THE SAME BRUSH SIZE AT VARYING ZOOM LEVELS..

20 » IT'S BEST TO COLOR OUTSIDE THE LINES.

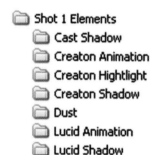

📁 Shot 1 Elements
   📁 Cast Shadow
   📁 Creaton Animation
   📁 Creaton Hightlight
   📁 Creaton Shadow
   📁 Dust
   📁 Lucid Animation
   📁 Lucid Shadow

21 » SAMPLE DIRECTORY STRUCTURE.

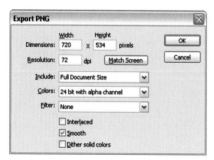

22 » THE PROPER EXPORT SETTINGS.

they'll be amplified with a glow, so keep their size to a minimum. **(SEE FIGURE 20.)**

:: LAYER EXODUS I

Flash doesn't make it simple to export elements. Use the following approach to export shots 1–5, and later you'll learn how to export the oversized animation in Shot 6. **(SEE FIGURE 21.)**

Create a folder on your hard drive for each layer to be exported. Then create a new Flash document with the same settings and create a new layer.

Switch back to the original file and select all the frames for the first layer to be exported. Copy the frames by pressing Cmd+Option+C (Ctrl+Alt+C).

Paste the frames in the top layer by pressing Cmd+Option+V (Ctrl+Alt+V).

1. Export a PNG image sequence by pressing Cmd+Option+S (Ctrl+Alt+S). Choose PNG Sequence. In the export PNG dialogue select Full Document Size and "24-bit with alpha channel."

Delete this newest layer and repeat the process until all the layers with animated elements are exported. **(SEE FIGURE 22.)**

:: GOODBYE, FLASH

It's time to make these shadows magic, so open After Effects and import the PNGs as sequences. Import the background PSD as a composition so that the layers come in separately. Delete the resulting composition. Create a new composition named Shot 1 using the NTSC DV 720X480 preset.

:: ADJUSTING THE FRAME RATE

After Effects has no way to decipher the proper frame rate of an image sequence and uses 30fps by default.

1. To fix this, select the first image sequence listed in the Project window and press Cmd+F (Ctrl+F) to bring up the Interpret Footage dialog.

2. Change the frame rate to 15fps.

3. To copy this setting and apply it to the other footage, with the sequences selected, press Cmd+Option+C (Ctrl+Alt+C).

4. Select the other image sequences and press Cmd+Option+V (Ctrl+Alt+V).

:: SET UP

Let's get our shot built.

1. Drag all the PNG sequences and background assets into Shot 1 and open the composition.

2. Press Cmd+K (Ctrl+K) to open the Composition Settings dialogue and adjust the Duration to match the length of your PNG sequences.

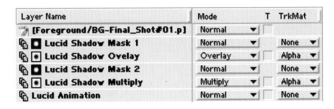

Layer Name	Mode	T	TrkMat
[Foreground/BG–Final_Shot#01.p]	Normal ▼		
🖿 ⬛ **Lucid Shadow Mask 1**	Normal ▼		None ▼
🖿 ⦿ **Lucid Shadow Ovelay**	Overlay ▼		Alpha ▼
🖿 ⦿ **Lucid Shadow Mask 2**	Normal ▼		None ▼
🖿 ⦿ **Lucid Shadow Multiply**	Multiply ▼		Alpha ▼
🖿 **Lucid Animation**	Normal ▼		None ▼

23 » THE DUAL LAYER APPROACH JUST BEFORE PRE-COMPOSITING.

TIP // **FLAG IT!** :: To label a frame, select it and open the Properties palette by pressing Cmd+F3 (Ctrl+F3). Enter the desired label in the text field "Frame." Use frame labels for marking the ends of animation cycles and production notes.

3. In your Timeline, move the sequences between the background and foreground layers of your scenery. Place Lucid's layers above Creaton's and each shadow layer above its counterpart.

4. Lastly, place the drop shadow below the other sequences and lock the background and foreground scenery layers.

:: DOUBLE UP

It's time to double-up some of our layers to achieve proper shading.

1. Select Lucid's shadow layer, rename it Lucid Shadow Multiply, and set the blending mode to Multiply.

2. Add the Tint effect (Effect>Image Control>Tint) and press F3 to open the Effects Controls. Select a dark purple for both "Map Black to" and "Map White to" and enter 100 for "Amount to Tint." This will create more appealing shadows.

3. Add a Gaussian Blur (Effect>Blur & Sharpen>Gaussian Blur) and in the Effect Controls, set the Blurriness to 5.

4. Next duplicate Lucid's layer (not his shadow) and name the duplicate Lucid Shadow Mask 1.

5. Place it above Lucid's shadow layer.

6. Set the Lucid Shadow Multiply layer's Track Matte to Alpha Matte.

7. Select both the shadow layer and the mask layer and duplicate them by pressing Cmd+D (Ctrl+D).

8. Rename the new shadow layer Lucid Shadow Overlay, switch its blending mode to Overlay, and increase the blur to 15. Lower the Lucid Shadow Multiply layer's opacity to 50. (SEE FIGURE 23.)

9. The idea is to use the multiplied shadow as the main shading and the overlay shadow to add depth and richness.

10. Finally, select all the layers related to Lucid and pre-compose them by pressing Cmd+Shift+C (Ctrl+Shift+C).

11. Repeat the process with Creaton and then the cast shadows. Choose a darker version of the predominant color of the element in the Tint effect. For Creaton it's dark brown and for the cast shadow it's dark green. (SEE FIGURE 24.)

12. Finish Creaton's eye highlights by adding a Gaussian Blur with the Blurriness set to 1.

13. Then add two separate Glow effects with parameters in FIGURE 25.

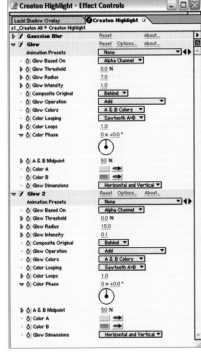

25 » THE DOUBLE GLOW EFFECT FOR HIGHLIGHTS.

24 » FLAT, SHADED, THEN GORGEOUS!

26 » ORIGINAL, WITH NOISE, AND BLUR.

27 » DRAG A RECTANGULAR MASK WITH PLENTY OF HEADROOM.

:: KICKING UP DUST

With a few simple adjustments, you can take the cartoonish, flat dust you animated and give it added vitality while complimenting the scenery.

1. First hide the character layers.

2. Select the Rectangular Mask Tool (Q) and click and drag a mask that starts at the bottom-left corner of the dust to twice its height above on the right side.

3. Then in the Mask properties (M), uncheck the lock aspect ratio on Mask Feather and set the vertical value to around 500, giving the dust a gradual fade.

4. Next add a Gaussian Blur with Blurriness set to 12.

5. Add the Noise effect at 25% and uncheck the Use Color Noise option. This will break up the flat areas of color.

6. Finally, an additional Gaussian Blur set to 5 is needed to soften the noise. (SEE FIGURE 26 & 27.)

:: RACK FOCUS

To achieve a simple switch in focus, we'll create a rack focus effect.

1. Create a new Adjustment Layer and place it below Lucid's layer. Name it Rack Focus BG.

2. Now add the Gaussian Blur effect to the new Adjustment Layer and Lucid's layer.

3. Set a key for the Blurriness just beyond one second into the shot, when Lucid nears the foreground.

4. Then at two seconds in, when Lucid pops up for his close-up, set another key and change the value to 15.

5. Set a keyframe for the Rack Focus BG layer's Blurriness and leave the value at 0.

6. Scrub forward in the Timeline about one second, just as Lucid settles from his pop. Set a key for both layers. For Lucid, change the value to 0, and for the Rack Focus BG layer set it at 3.

7. Now move forward to the point where Creaton charges into the clearing and switch the focus to the background using the same technique. (SEE FIGURE 28.)

:: 2 1/2 D LOOPING BACKGROUND

Remember watching "The Flintstones" as a kid and wondering why the exact same lamp kept flying by in the background? This will be similar, but not corny. For Shot 2, I'm going to show you how to take your layered seamless background and create depth by setting them in After Effect's 3D space.

:: PREPARING THE BACKGROUND

If you'd like to skip this step, locate the layered background files on the DVD accompanying this book and proceed to the next section. If not, you'll need to break up or organize your background into three layers using Photoshop:

Background: A completely opaque layer with low-detail trees and grass

Foreground: A layer of sporadic trees and grass

Ground: A layer of grass from a birds-eye view (SEE FIGURE 29.)

1. Run the Offset filter (Filter>Other>Offset) on each layer to center the seam.

2. Use the Clone tool or Healing Brush tool to blend away the seam on each layer.

3. On the Ground layer use a layer mask and the Gradient tool to fade the layer at the top so that it blends with the Foreground layer. Save your work and head to After Effects.

28 » THE RACK FOCUS EFFECT IN USE.

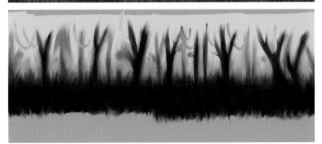
29 » THE THREE LAYERS OF THE CYCLE.

THE CHASE OF LUCID

BY **DAVE E. PHILLIPS**

MUSIC BY **CHRISTOPHER S. MURPHY**

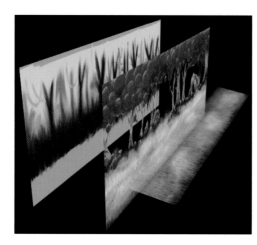

30 » THE SCENERY IN 3D SPACE.

:: SETTING THE STAGE

1. Create a new composition named Shot 2.

2. Import your PNG sequences and the background layers.

3. Change the PNG sequences' frame rate to 15fps.

4. Drag the elements into the Shot 2. Adjust the duration of the composition.

5. Finish off Lucid's shadows as previously described, pre-compose his layers and move the resulting layer to the top.

6. Turn on Motion Blur and 3D Layer for each background layer.

7. Hide Lucid's layer and switch the composition view from Active Camera to Custom View 3.

8. Then move the Background layer further back in on the Z-axis, just enough to achieve a little parallax.

9. Rotate the Ground layer −80° on the X-axis and adjust its position on the Z-axis so that it sits in front of the Foreground layer. Adjust its Y position so that the Ground ends just below the tree roots. Your result should look like **FIGURE** 31.

10. Select all three layers and pre-compose them.

11. Toggle on Collapse Transformations and 3D Layer for your new composition.

12. Switch the view back to Active Camera and unhide Lucid.

13. Next adjust the Y and Z position so that Lucid is placed in the proper position and scaled to the scenery.

:: MOVE IT

It's now time to put things into motion.

1. Duplicate the scenery layer and parent it to the original, linking the movement.

2. Now move the parent layer to the right until the edge of the layer is near the center of the composition.

3. Move the child layer left until its right edge is flush with the parent layer's left edge and thus seamless.

4. Now set the parent layer's X position at 0 and set a keyframe for position at frame 1. **(SEE FIGURE 31.)**

A few more nudges to the right, and seam will be hidden.

5. Move forward 10 or so frames and move the parent right until the child is framed as the parent is in frame 1.

6. Press J and K to toggle between the two keyframes to see the difference. Adjust the parent until the two key frames are identical.

:: TIME IT

Press 0 on the numeric keypad to see a RAM Preview. Chances are that the ground and Lucid aren't synced and Lucid appears to slide rather than run. Pick a visual landmark such as a tree in the background. Then adjust the second keyframe on the parent.

Find a spot where Lucid and your landmark are adjacent. Move ahead one or two frames, when Lucid's grounded foot has moved back. Is the spatial relationship the same with the foot and the landmark? If not, fine-tune the key frame until the relationship is consistent. Render another RAM Preview with Motion Blur enabled and watch closely. **(SEE FIGURE 32.)**

Did you catch it? The Motion Blur creates a seam where the two backgrounds connect. To correct this, move to a point in the cycle where the seam is centered in frame. Then nudge the child with right arrow key until it's once again seamless. Finally, adjust the second position key frame on the parent so that once again it is identical to frame 1.

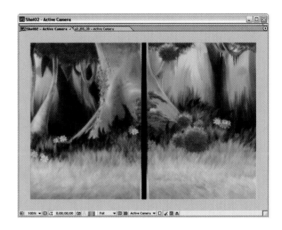

31 » **A FEW MORE NUDGES TO THE RIGHT, AND SEAM WILL BE HIDDEN.**

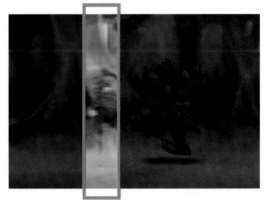

32 » **YIKES! THE MOTION BLUR EXPOSED THE SEAM.**

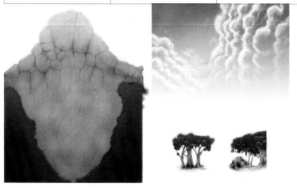

33 » IN THIS SHOT, THE STAR IS THE SCENERY.

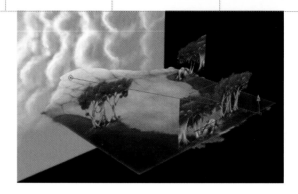

34 » THE ELEMENTS LAID OUT IN 3D SPACE.

:: LOOP IT

Let's save some time by looping our animation.

1. **To make a seamless loop, select both scenery layers, pre-compose them and open the resulting comp.**

2 **In the Composition Settings adjust the duration of the comp so that it ends one frame earlier than the last-position keyframe on the parent layer.**

3. **Return to Shot 2 and click RAM Preview.**

There's one last issue. Lucid's PNG sequence is running at 15fps, but the cycle is running at 29.97fps. Notice that every other frame, the ground slips past Lucid. In other words, the background is too smooth. To fix this simply add the Posterize Time effect to the cycle layer and enter 15 for the Frame Rate. Finally, duplicate the cycle in the Timeline to run the length of the shot.

:: HAND-HELD CAMERA

Shot 5 is Lucid's point of view approaching the precipice. Here you'll employ a simple hand-held camera effect. It consists of setting up scenery image planes in 3D space, flying a camera through the scene and then giving it some wiggle.

:: THE CAST

This shot has two stars: the ground and the sky. The ground should be drawn like Figure 33. I've created mine at 2460X3170 pixels. This will provide plenty of resolution for when a portion of the plane is close to the camera. On the layer below the ground create a cloudy blue sky.

The supporting cast of the shot is the trees, rocks, and shrubs. Simply nab two samples of trees from the Foreground layer of Shot 2. In Photoshop, use the Eraser tool to quickly blend out the bottom grass edges and the Clone tool to finish off the top tree leaves that were cut off. **(SEE FIGURE 33.)**

:: THE SET

It's time to finish off this set for our next shot.

1. **In After Effects, create a new composition named Shot 5.**

2. **Change the duration to four seconds.**

3. **Import the background PSD using the Composition—Cropped Layers option.**

4. **Delete the resulting comp and drag the scene elements into Shot 5.**

5. **Toggle on Motion Blur and 3D Layer options for all layers then hide the tree layers.**

6. **Create a new camera with the 35mm preset named Main Camera.**

7. **Next rotate the Ground layer –90° on the X-axis.**

8. **Move the sky layer back on the Z-axis until it completely clears the cliff, then scale it up to approximately two times the size of the frame.**

9. **Switch the composition view to Custom View 3 and turn back on the tree layers.**

10. **Duplicate and position your trees so that they then resemble those in FIGURE 34.**

:: KEY THE CAMERA

1. **Position the camera at the front edge of the Ground layer and the camera's Point of Interest at the opposite end of the layer but just below it.**

2. **Keyframe both attributes and then move to the end of the Timeline.**

3. **Position the camera near the cliff edge, lower it on the Y-axis, and adjust your Point of Interest to better frame the shot. Then tweak the camera's path handles to form a nice arc to the descent. (SEE FIGURE 35.)**

35 » THE POSITION OF THE CAMERA, VIEWED FROM THE LEFT.

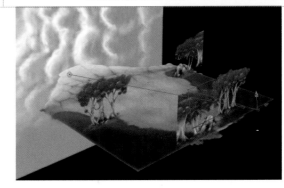

36 » THE WIGGLER PANEL.

:: JUST WIGGLE IT

1. Select both keyframes for the camera position and launch The Wiggler panel (Window>The Wiggler).

2. Select Spatial Path and the Smooth noise type. Click the All Dimensions Independently radio button and enter 10 for the Frequency and 40 for the Magnitude.

3. Click Apply.

4. Now select both key frames for the camera's Point of Interest.

5. In The Wiggler panel choose One Dimension and select Y from the drop-down menu.

6. Enter 5 for the Frequency and 15 for the Magnitude and click Apply.

7. Lastly, open the Composition Settings and click the Advanced tab. Enter 400 for the Shutter Angle and click OK.

8. RAM Preview to test the results. (SEE FIGURE 36.)

Traditional Camera Moves

:: LAYER EXODUS II

In Shot 6 you'll learn how to quickly create a traditional boom, track, and dolly using After Effect's 3D space. First in Flash, you'll need to export your oversized animation for this shot. The major steps you'll need to complete are:

1. Open the FLA in file and resave it with a new name.

2. Strip the file of all scenes except for the one containing Shot 6.

3. Delete unanimated layers.

4. Increase the document size to the size of your artwork (2400X2000).

5. Then turn on the Edit Multiple Frames option and under Modify Onion Markers select Onion All.

6. Select everything and move it to the center of the stage. Turn off Edit Multiple Frames.

7. Change every layer except the top layer into a Guide Layer.

8. Export an appropriately named PNG sequence as before.

9. Change the recently exported layer into a Guide Layer and switch the layer below back to a normal layer.

10. Export and repeat.

:: SETUP

1. In After Effects, create a new composition named Shot 6.

2. Import your PNG sequences and import your background Photoshop file as composition.

3. Change the PNG sequences' frame rate to 15fps.

4. Delete the resulting composition and drag all the elements into Shot 6.

5. Change the duration of the composition to that of the PNG sequences and order the layers appropriately.

6. Next create a new Null Object (Layer>New>Null Object) named All Assets.

7. Parent all the other layers to this null object.

8. Move All Assets so that the cliff edge is viewable and go forward in the Timeline to when Lucid is crouched down at the edge with his fingers overlapping the rock face. Select all the animated layers and position them so that Lucid is properly registered with the cliff face.

9. Scale All Assets down so that you can see most of the scene. Finish the shadows and dust using the techniques learned earlier.

10. Use a duplicate of the cliff layer as a track matte for the cast shadows.

THE MUSIC MAN

» HERE'S CHRIS IN HIS STUDIO CREATING THE SCORE.

Christopher S. Murphy of www.farawaynearby.com is the genius behind the musicial score for this sequence. If you haven't already, pop in the DVD and listen to it. What is especially impressive is that the rich sound of a full orchestra was created in his small studio with a MIDI keyboard! Christopher used Steinberg's Cubase SX to record, sequence and produce the score. In addition, he used an orchestral plug-in to drive the VST instruments in the score. So before you reach for that bargain-rack royalty-free music CD, consider finding a talented guy like Chris to tailor a score to your piece. It's an added line in the budget, but catapults the feel of your piece from good to glorious.

Before implementing the camera move, you need to address one issue. Lucid and Creaton pass from one side of the cliff to the other. So for both characters, you'll need to split the layer at the transition (Cmd+D for Mac, Ctrl+D for PC) and sandwich the foremost cliff layer between the two.

Select all the PNG layers and the foremost cliff layer and pre-compose them. Within the new composition, increase the size in the Composition Settings until all artwork fits comfortably in the frame. Return to Shot 6. (SEE FIGURE 37.)

:: MAKE YOUR (CAMERA) MOVE

Toggle on 3D Layer and Motion Blur for all the layers in Shot 6. Stagger the layers along the Z-axis starting from front to back. Give just enough space to give a noticeable parallax while moving. You can test it by grabbing the All Assets layer and moving it around.

1. Reposition All Assets so that the cliff edge is framed for the first part of the shot.

2. Scrub through the track up to Creaton's fall to make sure all action stays in frame. Then around eight seconds, after Creaton has fallen out of frame, set a keyframe for both position and rotation.

3. Go forward two seconds. Frame the shot on Lucid hanging from the branch by repositioning All Assets and rotating it clockwise.

4. Dolly in by moving All Assets towards the camera on the Z-axis.

5. Select all key frames and press F9 to apply Easy Ease.

6. Finally, move to the end of the composition and move All Assets the tiniest bit closer to camera.

7. Click RAM Preview, and you should see the camera boom down, track right, and dolly in followed by a subtle dolly in.

:: FILL THE GAPS

Now it's time to use what you've learned to finish Shots 3 and 4. In Shot 3, all the elements are animated frame by frame. All you'll need to do is set them up in Flash, export them and finish the shadows in After Effects.

Shot 4 is simply a close-up of Lucid running. Recycle the looping background you created earlier by scaling it up and adding a generous Gaussian Blur.

:: RENDER AND EDIT

Once you've completed all the shots, I recommend rendering them individually before you edit them together in After Effects. Render using a lossless codec (such as Animation) so that you maintain the quality in the edit. Then you can sequence the shots in a new composition. Add an opacity fade-out at the end of Shot 6.

:: AUDIO

Audio will make or break your animation. Many great tools exist including Sony Vegas for the PC platform and Soundtrack Pro for the Mac platform. Both offer the ability to score to picture and add sound effects.

However most great animators are not also composers. I had the good fortune to know an amazing musician who created a custom score to the animation. So simply import the music from the accompanying DVD and place it in the Timeline to see and hear what a difference music makes.

:: HIDING THE EVIDENCE

You've completed the sequence but it still looks like Flash! To keep you from being accused of putting web toons on television, I've gathered a few tips to hide your animation's origin and make it broadcast safe.

:: WORKING DIRTY

The dead giveaway that this sequence is Flash-based is ultra-clean artwork. So make it dirty.

Create a new Adjustment Layer named Soft Focus and add a 15-pixel Gaussian Blur. Lower the layer opacity to 30%.

Create another Adjustment Layer named Video Blur, add a 1-pixel Gaussian Blur but only vertically. This will reduce flickering on video from thin line weights.

Now add a new Solid Layer filled with 50% gray and name it Noise. Apply the Add Noise effect with the default settings and reduce the layer opacity to 50%. This effect will break up the telltale flat color and bring it closer to the look of film.

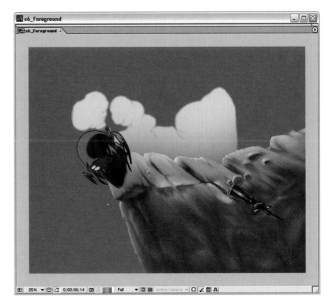

37 » RESIZE THE FOREGROUND COMPOSITION TO THE SIZE OF THE ARTWORK.

38 » FROM BEGINNING TO END. A LITTLE AFTER EFFECTS GOES A LONG WAY.

Add yet another Solid Layer named Film Edge and choose black as the fill color. Double-click the Elliptical Mask tool to create an elliptical mask the exact size of the layer. Then in the Mask settings, invert the mask, increase the feathering to 200 and the expansion to 100. This effect mimics the way old films darken around the edges.

Add one more Adjustment Layer named Video Levels and add the Levels effect. Set the Output Black to 16 and the Output White to 235. This will bring your animation into the video-safe range. If you have extremely vivid colors, you may consider adding a Hue/Saturation effect and lowering the saturation.

Finally select all these effect layers and pre-compose them, making sure to turn on Collapse Transformations afterwards.

Now you have a portable effect that you can add to any other scene in an animation or duplicate and make variations. One possibility is a web variation. Just duplicate the composition and delete the two video-safe layers. (SEE FIGURE 38.)

Conclusion

Well, you did it. You produced a whopping 45 seconds of broadcast-quality animation! I hope I've shown you at least a few new tricks and that you can produce beautiful broadcast-quality animation on a budget. Good luck, and may your audience love your ones, accept your twos and forgive your threes.

ABOUT THE AUTHOR

Dave E. Phillips is best known for saturating the web with his subversively humorous animated Flash shorts. He began his career in fine art but soon felt the pull of animation. Since completing a degree in 2D and 3D animation, Dave has assisted in the creation of animation and motion graphics pieces for clients such as the American Diabetes Association and America Online. Dave currently resides in the Albany, NY area with his wife, Amy.

ABOUT THE PROJECT

This animated sequence was fully animated and produced by Dave E. Phillips. It was created as an accompaniment to a production bible for "Lucid the Dreamer." In order to attract network attention, Dave wanted to create a compelling and visually stunning sequence that would immediately immerse viewers in Lucid's dream world. He has met that goal by combining the best aspects of Flash and After Effects.

Photo by Amy Phillips

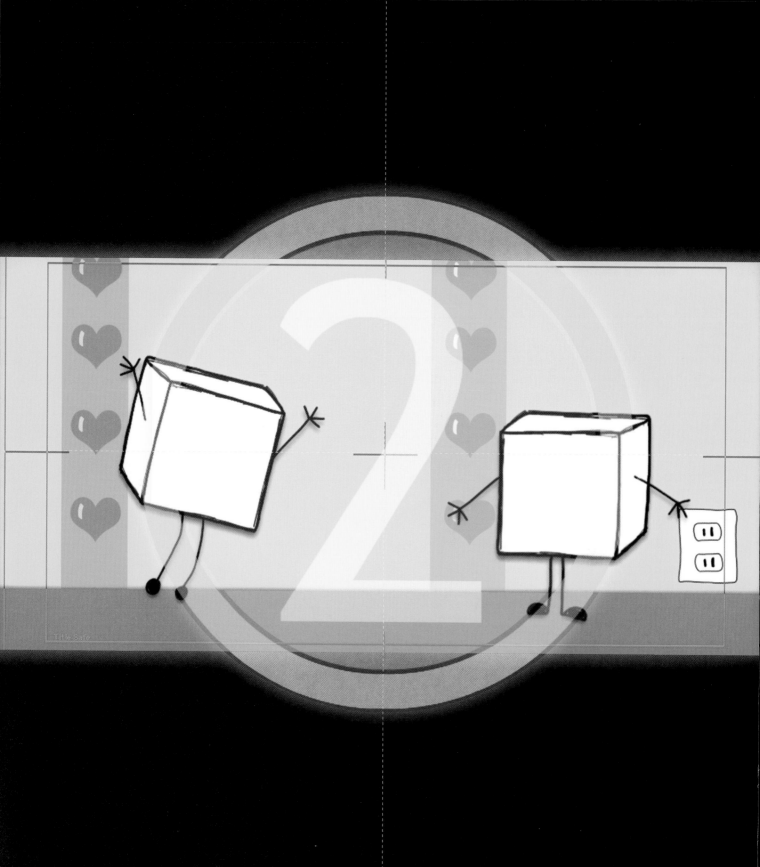

ANIMATING FOR FILM: DIGITAL TO ANALOG

RACHEL MAX

Creating a high-resolution cut-out animation in After Effects for output to 35mm film

HOW THE PROJECT ORIGINATED :: In 2000 I screened a short animation at the Slamdance Film Festival and began my love affair with the film festival circuit, Slamdance, and animating quirky, low-fi shorts. :: Slamdance is the notorious "other" film festival in Park City, Utah which runs concurrently to Sundance. Started in 1996 by Independent filmmakers who didn't get into Sundance, Slamdance ("by filmmakers, for filmmakers!") supports first-time direc- tors with films funded by the generosity of friends, family, and high-interest-rate credit cards. Every year the Slamdancers face the challenge of putting together another amaz- ing festival and delicately choose a small percentage of their submissions to be screened.

One of the many things to be done in preparation for the festival is creating the official trailer that runs before each screening. The trailer showcases the festival sponsors and brands the look of the festival. The festival directors have taken a creative approach to the trailer design by handing it off to a different alumnus each year. In 2003 they called me. :: In this chapter, I'll discuss aspects of how I made the trailer. I'll also address film aspect ratios and how to do cut-out style animation in After Effects.

WHAT'S ON THE DVD
The DVD contains the 2003 Slamdance Film Festival trailer, as well as an After Effects project and the artwork used to create the trailer. These sources are copyright Slamdance, Eighteenth Street Lounge, and Rachel Max, and are not to be reused in any form.

01 » SLAMDANCE HEADQUARTERS AT THE TREASURE MOUNTAIN INN

Concept

I was told the theme that year was innocence and getting back to basics. The festival was moving from a large abandoned silver mine it had used for two years back to the Treasure Mountain Inn on the top of Main Street where the festival started. **(SEE FIGURE 01.)**

A graphic artist from Los Angeles had been chosen to design the programs, and the director thought my style of animation would work well for the trailer. It was the beginning of what Indiewire later described as "a wonderful, crudely animated festival trailer." Sweet!

I was living next door to some cute kids at the time, and I thought it would be great to get them involved. I came up with the idea of involving children in a classroom, somehow mistaking the Slamdance logo for a shape. It would be animated with voice-over from a video shoot with the children.

I asked a friend to help me, and we arranged to shoot at the neighbor's house. There was no budget for the trailer, so I borrowed a GL1 and shot using just the mic on the camera. Lighting wasn't an issue since we only needed the audio. The hardest part of the shoot was getting performances from the children. It took about three hours, but we got enough for the short trailer.

At the time I started this project I was working with After Effects 5.5 on a dual-processor 800 MHz G4 running Mac OS 10.2. I was still transitioning to OS X and was running some software in OS 9. I edited the footage with Apple Final Cut Pro 3 and narrowed down the audio clips I wanted. I output stereo 44.1kHz, 16-bit AIFF files from Final Cut Pro and edited them in Macromedia SoundEdit 16. I normalized the levels and edited out digital pops.

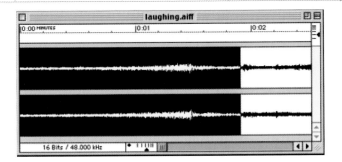

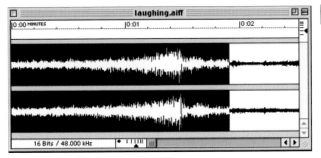

02 & 03 » COMPARE THE AUDIO WAVEFORM BEFORE AND AFTER NORMALIZATION.

Recording audio with a GL1 meant there was a lot of over-modulation. I saved the edited AIFF files as .mov files and assembled the audio in After Effects. **(SEE FIGURE 02 & 03.)**

For corporate work I would usually opt to use music from a music stock library (see Chris and Trish Meyer's chapter for more information on stock music), but I was on a mission to use a song called "Margaret Evening Fashion" by a German group called Le Hammond Inferno. I first heard the song on a CD called *All Systems Are Go Go* put out by the DJ Ursula 1000 and Eighteenth Street Lounge Music. I love the upbeat-retro-electronic sound of the album. My search led me to Le Hammond Inferno record label Bungalow in Berlin. I was told that there were some unresolved issues with the song which prevented its use but that they would gladly put me in touch with Ursula 1000.

You never know what people are willing to give you until you ask. A week later, after a lovely phone call with Alex Gimeno of Ursula, I licensed the song "Beatbox Cha Cha" from his album *Kinda Kinky*. Slamdance is a non-profit and couldn't offer monetary compensation for the use of the song, but the festival has a large worldwide audience so it was good exposure for the artist. **(SEE FIGURE 04.)**

04 » THE KINDA KINKY ALBUM COVER COURTESY OF ESL MUSIC AND URSULA 1000

Delivery Specs

To begin a project you have to understand where it's going. I needed to know the delivery specs before I could begin to draw. Slamdance was being sponsored in part by The Digital Film Group from Vancouver, which specializes in converting video and digital files to 35mm film. They use only true film resolution film recorders and are known for their beautiful crisp transfers of films like *The Corporation* and *Atanarjuat: the Fast Runner*.

06 » SOME RATIOS COMPARED
COURTESY OF THE DIGITAL
FILM GROUP

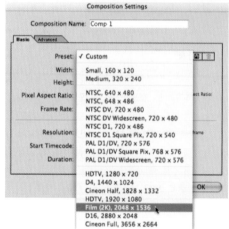

05 » THE DEFAULT 2K RESOLUTION IN AFTER EFFECTS

The default 2K composition size in After Effects is 2048x1536, which is 4x3, or a 1.33:1 ratio, and known in the film world as Academy Standard. **(SEE FIGURE 05.)**

The 1.33:1 ratio was the standard for films made up until the early 1950s. It was also the ratio the National Television Standards Committee (NTSC) chose during the advent of TV because it permitted the most efficient use of motion picture film. During the late 1950s Hollywood changed film sizes to draw the TV audience back to the cinemas. The two most common newer ratios are 1.85:1, known as Academy Flat and 2.35:1, known as Anamorphic Scope. Less-used film ratios are 1.66:1 and 2.20:1 (70mm). The ratio of 1.78:1, otherwise known as 16x9, was one of these less-used ratios, but we will see more of it as it is the proposed standard for HDTV. **(SEE FIGURE 06.)**

The lab informed me that the ratio was going to be 1.85:1 or a composition size of 2048x1107 pixels. The delivery specs for the project were to be:

• an uncompressed TARGA sequence

• Universal Leader at the head of the trailer

• a frame of 1000Hz tone at the 2 during the leader
  (creates what's known as the 2 pop)

• a tail pop five seconds after last frame of action (LFOA)

The project settings were 24fps, 35mm, in 8-bit color space. I had previously exported the audio files from Final Cut Pro as 44.1kHz, so I decided to stick with that. Keeping the audio at the original 48kHz would have been slightly better, but I didn't have the time to re-export and re-optimize the audio. **(SEE FIGURE 07.)**

The Universal Leader, also known as the Academy Leader, is usu-

07 » THE PROJECT SETTINGS

10 »   THE SPARKY AWARD COURTESY OF KARIN HAYES

09 »

ally used to provide projectionists with information like the name of the work and to cue when sound and picture actually start. It also protects the film from being handled and allows the projector to get up to full speed before the film begins. In this case, the Digital Film Group also needed the leader with 1000kHz pops to sync the sound to the picture. The sound and picture go through several stages before they are married in a composite film print and are synced at the 2 during the leader to the one frame of 1000kHz tone in the audio track. Including the tail pop is a step usually done for feature films, but it helps a projectionist using a platter system to know when a film has ended. **(SEE FIGURE 08.)**

Asset Management

One reason I love animation is that you can create your own assets at any point in the production. Production and postproduction get meshed together, which solves many problems and of course creates others. I didn't have a tremendous amount of time at this point, and ironically I don't draw very well. The first thing I set about drawing was the Slamdance mascot Sparky. **(SEE FIGURE 09.)**

When in doubt, trace. I brought a low-resolution JPEG into an arbitrarily high-resolution Photoshop image that was 2036X1719 pixels. I scaled the JPEG to fit and then used the Brush tool to outline Sparky. I painted dabs of color on his face and went back and forth between Photoshop 7 and Corel Painter 7 to blend the colors. Open the file Sparky.psd from this chapter's footage folder on the DVD enclosed with this book. **(SEE FIGURE 10.)**

You'll notice that I have four layers. **(SEE FIGURE 11.)**

I have a layer for Sparky's face, a layer of extra lines (I wasn't sure if I wanted that effect or not), and individual layers for his left and right eyelids so I could make him blink and wink when I got to the

08 »   PICTURE START ON UNIVERSAL LEADER

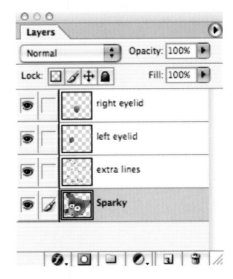

11 »

» THE PLATTER PROJECTION SYSTEM AT THE AFI SILVER THEATER
COURTESY OF GABE WARDELL

PREVIEW A SEGMENT

To preview a segment of the final movie, press a number such as 1 (on the standard keyboard, not the numeric keypad) to jump to that marker, press B to set the start of the work area to that point, press a later number such as 2 to jump to that marker, press N to end the work area, and then press 0 on the numeric keypad to RAM Preview that segment. You can also use Page Up and Page Down to step through the piece frame by frame.

12 »

13 »

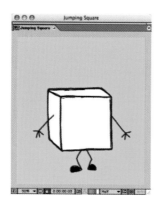

14 »

15 »

animation stage. When working with cut-outs I put everything that can be animated on separate layers. We'll look at more detailed files and talk about animating them later in the chapter.

Next I drew a chalkboard for the classroom setting and a few shapes that the kids were going to confuse with the Slamdance logo. I started in Photoshop and made a new image that would match the 2048x1107 size of the final animation. Open Chalkboard.psd to see the results. (SEE FIGURE 12.)

It's a good thing I'm not a primary school teacher because as you'll notice my alphabet ends at W. I got to W and realized that although film doesn't have title-safe and action-safe areas, video does, and this trailer was going on the annual Slamdance DVD. It looks a bit weird to me now but at the time I probably had a good reason for not resizing the alphabet banner and adding XYZ.

Open other files from the Artwork folder. You'll notice that the shape files have many layers as all their legs are on separate layers. Let discuss why I set up my files like this and how to animate a jumping square.

Tutorial: Animating the Jumping Square

Open Slamdance Trailer 2003.aep. In the Project window, open the Renders folder and double-click on Jumping Square.mov to play the file. At the top of the Project window, you should see information about the file such as its size, the fact that it has an alpha channel and that it is used twice. (SEE FIGURE 13.)

Now go to the Precomps folder in the Comps folder and open Jumping Square. (SEE FIGURE 14.)

Select all the layers in the Timeline by pressing Cmd-A (Ctrl-A) and press U to view all the keyframes in the composition.(SEE FIGURE 15.)

LINKS TO GREAT MUSIC

Ursula 1000: www.ursula1000.com

Eighteenth Street Lounge: www.eslmusic.com

Bungalow Records: www.bungalow.de

MUSIC LICENSING

Music licensing can be tricky because you need to obtain both the performance rights and the publishing rights. For this reason I choose to approach an independent label. If you can't afford a lawyer to draft a contract, there are books that come with examples of various production forms. I recommend *The Complete Film Production Handbook* by Eve Light Honthaner. It is designed for feature film production, but much of it can be applied to commercials, promos, and most any creative work.

These are Hold Keyframes meaning that there is no interpolation between the action, so the animation is sudden. It makes for jumpy but cute and disarming animations. In the Project window, open the Tutorials folder and double-click the Jumping Square *Start* composition. **(SEE FIGURE 16.)**

Looking at the layers, you'll notice I switched the position of legs7 and legs8 because the new order looked better. Make sure your Parent column is visible. If it's not, Ctrl-click (right-click) on the top of any column and select it. **(SEE FIGURE 17.)**

Hold down the Cmd (Ctrl) key and select layers 1, 2, 3, and 5. In the Parent column use the pickwhip or click on the bar and parent the layers to layer 4, "clean square." **(SEE FIGURE 18.)**

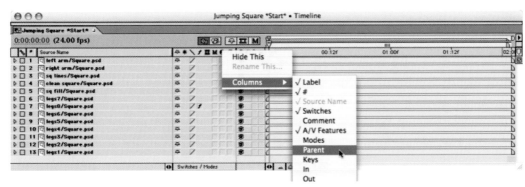

17 »

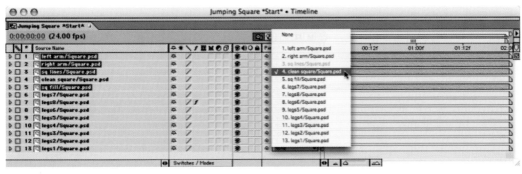

18 »

⚙ **KEEPING THE FILL SEPARATE**

You'll notice in many of the comps and in the original Photoshop artwork that I kept the fill colors separate from the outline of the shapes. I did this so I could change the color of any of the layers with the Fill effect keeping my options open for background colors. In the Project window, go to the Precomps folder in the Comps folder and open the Heart composition. Select the line layer and press E to show all applied effects. The Fill effect is filling the original black outline of the heart with white.

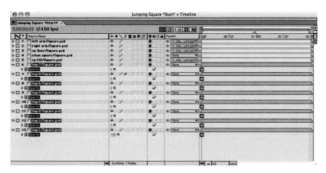

19 »

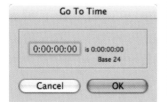

20 » YOU CAN TYPE A FRAME NUMBER

21 » YOU CAN MOVE A SPECIFIC NUMBER OF FRAMES.

Select layers 6 through 13, press T to show Opacity and set keyframes on these layers by clicking and dragging the mouse over each stopwatch. **SEE FIGURE 19.)**

Move forward three frames and set a keyframe for legs1 at 0% opacity and legs2 at 100% opacity. The premise here is that only one leg layer is visible at a time. Continue to set opacity keyframes for each of the leg layers every three frames until all the layers have been animated coming on and off. As you set the leg keyframe, position layer 4 correctly to match the leg position. To move three frames at a time you can scrub in the Timeline or click on the timecode bar in the Timeline window, press the + sign on your numeric keypad, enter the number 3, and press return to move ahead three keyframes. This also works in reverse by entering + –3 (or however many keyframes). **(SEE FIGURES 20, 21 & 22.)**

When you get to frame 15 and have set opacity keyframes for layers 8 through 13 and position keyframes for layer 4, scrub back through your animation. Your keyframes are linear, so the opacity changes are interpolated. It should look a bit like the bionic man in slow motion. We'll change this in a minute. **(SEE FIGURE 23.)**

23 »

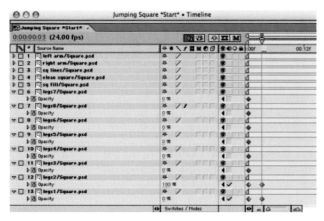

22 » BEGINNING TO SET OPACITY KEYFRAMES EVERY THREE FRAMES.

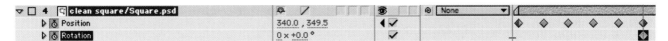

24 »

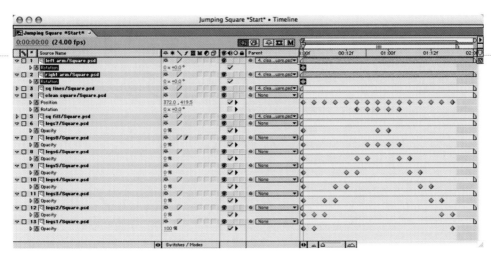

25 »   SETTING ROTATION KEYFRAMES FOR THE ARMS AT 0:00

Let's continue setting the keyframes. Go back to frame 15. Select layer 4, hold the Shift key and press R to bring up Rotation. Click the stopwatch to set a keyframe at 0° rotation. **(SEE FIGURE 24.)**

Move to frame 18, set opacity keyframes for layers 7 and 8 and set another position keyframe for layer 4. This time also set a rotation keyframe of 8°. Move forward to frame 21 and set opacity keyframes for layers 6 and 7 and this time set your rotation for layer 4 to 19°. This is the top of the jump. From here on you'll be setting keyframes for the descent of the square. When you get to 1:18 make sure the position and rotation values for layer 4 match the values at the beginning of the composition. The easy way to do this is select the position keyframe at 0:00, press Cmd-C (Ctrl-C) to copy it, make sure you're at 1:18, select layer 4, and paste the keyframe by pressing Cmd-V (Ctrl-V). Now you have a complete loop.

Next you need to keyframe the rotation on the arms. Press the Home key to go to the beginning of the composition. Select layers 1 and 2 and bring up Rotation (press R). **(SEE FIGURE 25.)**

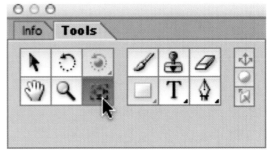

26 »

Make sure the anchor points are at the bottom of the arms where they connect with the body. Use the Pan Behind tool to move them to the correct position if not. **(SEE FIGURE 26.)**

When people jump, their arms start out by their sides and then rotate up until they are above their heads at the highest point of the jump. We'll use that same principle here. At 0:00 set a keyframe at layer 1 at –76 degrees and layer 2 at 92 degrees (or whatever you think best). Continue through the Timeline setting keyframes,

27 »

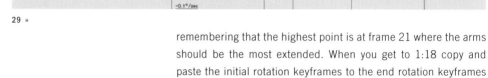

28 »

29 »

remembering that the highest point is at frame 21 where the arms should be the most extended. When you get to 1:18 copy and paste the initial rotation keyframes to the end rotation keyframes to sustain your loop.

Select all your keyframes by clicking and dragging over them all. Select Animation>Toggle Hold Keyframe or press Cmd-Opt-H (Ctrl-Alt-H). (SEE FIGURE 27.)

Your keyframes will go from linear interpolation to no interpolation. (SEE FIGURE 28 & 29.)

At 1:18 press N to end your work. Press the Home key to return to the beginning, and press B to begin the work area here. Choose Composition>Make Movie or press Cmd-M (Ctrl-M) to make a movie. (SEE FIGURE 30.)

For Render Settings choose Best Settings and for the Output Module select Lossless with Alpha. (SEE FIGURE 31.)

30 »

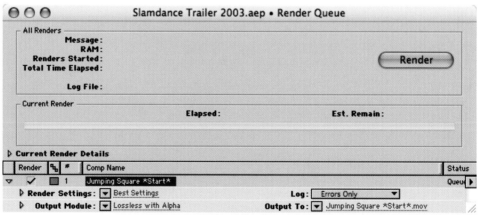

31 »

78

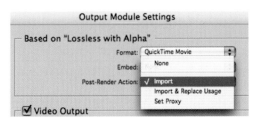

32 »

33 »

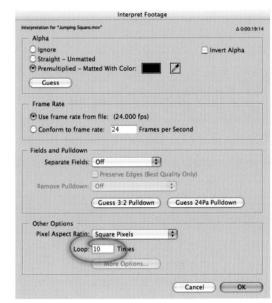

34 »

Click on Lossless with Alpha and change Post-Render Action to Import so After Effects will import the rendered file. Render your file. **(SEE FIGURE 32.)**

Once the file is rendered and has been imported, Ctrl-click (right-click) on the file in the Project window and select Interpret Footage. You could have also selected the file and pressed Cmd-F (Ctrl-F). **(SEE FIGURE 33.)**

In the Loop field change enter 10. **(SEE FIGURE 34.)**

You can now use this file in any composition without having to set all those keyframes. There are other ways we could have achieved the same result. We could have used expressions to loop the cycle, but I find that rendering QuickTime files improves overall speed. I am working with a 1GHz PowerBook now and need to cut as many corners as I can.

Open the "background for squares" composition in the Precomps folder to see the looped Jumping Square.mov in action. **(SEE FIG-URE 35.)**

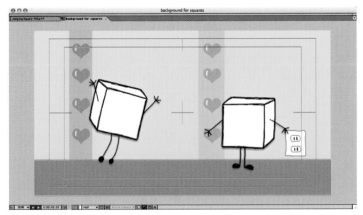

35 »

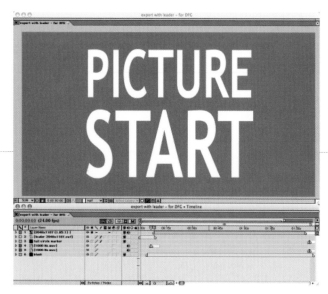

36 »

37 »

From the Computer to the Silver Screen

I assembled the compositions in a main composition called 2048x1107 and then placed that comp in a final export comp called Export With Leader, where I added the Universal Leader and the 1000Hz tones. **(SEE FIGURE 36.)**

I had to be careful to have the 1000Hz tone on only one frame. If the tone extended more than one frame the lab wouldn't have been able to find the sync mark. It was also imperative to have the first frame of action 48 frames after the 2 Pop. **(SEE FIGURE 37.)**

I rendered a smaller 720x540 version of the trailer starting at the 2 Pop so the lab could compare their sync to my version. The deliverables were a complete TARGA sequence, an AIFF file, and a smaller rendered QuickTime of the trailer. I sent these on a small FireWire drive which Digital Film Group would send back after they were done. They recorded the TARGA sequence to film and had the audio converted at a sound house. The converted audio was married back to the picture later in a composite print. The optical audio track on a 35mm print is always 21 frames in advance of the picture due to light traveling faster than sound. They made several prints from that composite print and sent them to Slamdance.

The festival was a great success, and the trailer went over well. I strongly recommend going out to Park City, Utah during the festivals and watching as many films as you can—especially the short films.

For a list of film festivals near you go to:

www.filmfestivals.com.

ABOUT THE AUTHOR

Rachel Max has been writing and animating short films for seven years and has been showing them in film festivals internationally since 1999. Her work has been broadcast on HBO, IFC, the Sundance Channel, and most recently on the show "Jump Cuts" on Comedy Central. Her clients include GEICO, Apple Computer, Bright Eyes, Slamdance, and MTV. She lives in New York City where she works as a freelance broadcast designer, producer, and teacher.

SOFTWARE AND HARDWARE USED

Shot with a Canon GL1

Digitized and edited with Final Cut Pro 3

Audio edited in SoundEdit 16 and Peak

Drawings done in Painter 7 and Photoshop 7

Input device was a Wacom Intuos 2 Graphics Tablet 6x8

Resolution was 2048x1107

Composited in After Effects 5.5

Output as a TARGA sequence

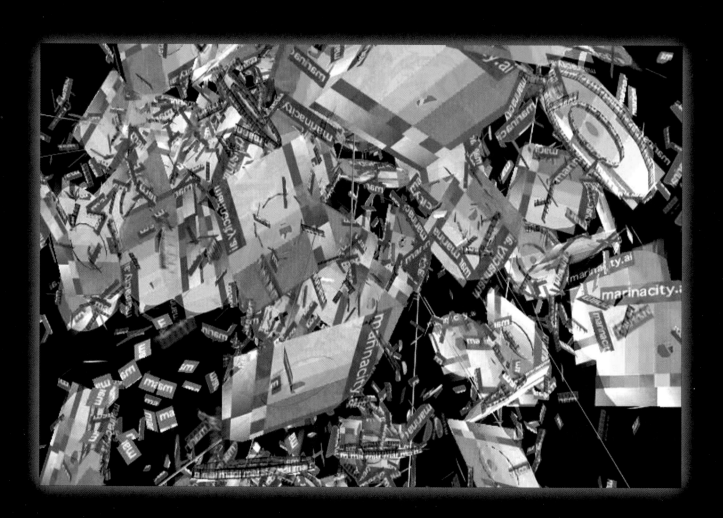

CHICAGO MOTION GRAPHICS

BY MASON DIXON, DESIGN AFTER NEXT

From Kansas City to Chicago to Detroit, the Midwest has been blossoming with creative video works: slick animations, seductive commercials, beautiful shorts, dancing-head music videos, 2D cutouts and illegal cutups. The vast majority are going unnoticed, unscreened, or scattered among festivals stubbornly clinging to genre barriers: animation vs. film, art vs. advertising. So in 2003 the Chicago Motion Graphics Festival was founded to collect and celebrate the best video works emerging in between 3D animation and traditional editing.

The opening for the 2003 festival had a special challenge: to intrigue a room of motion graphics artists while setting itself apart from the rest of the commercials, music videos, films, and artworks shown that night.

WHAT'S ON THE DVD
Included on the DVD are all of the source files for the project and a completed rendered sequence.

One of the first things motion graphics designers will criticize about other people's work is the use of effects. There is a sense that effects are shortcuts for more complicated tricks created by artists who were being more innovative. Of course, not all effects and plug-ins produce cheap imitations of masterworks, but it seemed like pure animation would be more striking than an effects-based approach.

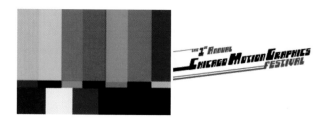

Tools:

Adobe After Effects, Photoshop, and Illustrator; Curious Labs' Poser; and Digidesign's Pro Tools

Budget:

Daily Planet, Creamy Orange, and Design After Next donated the time of their motion designers. The effort totaled over 200 hours and would have billed at over $18,000.

Main Concepts:

- Using the Rotate Camera tool

- Enhancing perspective distortion with depth

- Using Anchor Point to quickly make 3D models

- Mixing 2D and 3D objects in a convincing composition

- Storyboarding for quality and speed

- Using flowcharts to structure 3D compositions

 HALF OF MOTION IS SOUND

The final piece has a soundtrack that is tightly integrated with the visuals. This is one of the aspects that makes the piece so effective. In most projects an audio track is selected and visuals are composed to match. For this piece, the animation was created first and the audio track was composed later in Pro Tools.

Poser was used to make still images of people. Several images were combined in sequences to create walk cycles and other movements

Exploring the Project

Open ChicagoMotionGraphics.aep, locate CMGF.mov, and double-click its icon in the Project window. Play the movie and pause every few seconds. Look at each individual element used to make a scene. This study will focus on the first sequence in which color bars fall away to reveal the city of Chicago. Open 1-Final Project by double-clicking on it in the Project window. Referring to the comp markers, here are a few of the highlights:

(1) Color Bars: This image, familiar to most video professionals, becomes the image that is matched at the beginning of the camera move.

(2) People: Image sequences were imported to create a group of people outlines that could walk through the streets of our constructed city. They are the first and one of the most important details used to make this animation convincing.

(3) Buildings: A first set of buildings draws on with a set of animated masks, while more buildings appear in the background.

(4) City: By the end of the camera move a full city is revealed with hundreds of buildings shown. While the city appears to be fully three-dimensional, the majority of the buildings are flat, two-dimensional photos. These photos are placed to reinforce the illusion of the city. The majority of these photos were prepared in either Photoshop or Illustrator and were imported as multilayer documents.

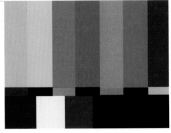

01 » THE COLOR BARS

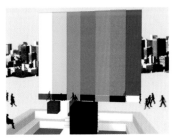

02 » PEOPLE

03 » BUILDINGS

04 » FULL CITY

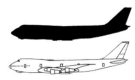

05 » SOURCE FILES

06 » SOURCE FILES

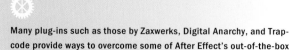

When creating Illustrator files for import as a multilayer document, be sure to put each object on a separate layer, and each layer at the top of the layer order. Layers within layers are not yet supported for Illustrator import.]

Many plug-ins such as those by Zaxwerks, Digital Anarchy, and Trapcode provide ways to overcome some of After Effect's out-of-the-box limitations by curving object surfaces, creating smoke, and arranging large 3D structures with many unique parts.

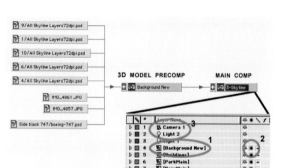

07 » SHOWING THE CONNECTION BETWEEN PRECOMPS USED AS 3D MODELS AND THE ANIMATIONS COMPS THEY ARE USED INSIDE OF.

Tutorial 1 : Building a Building

After Effects provides a simplified 3D toolset that is designed to lend itself to the type of work that motion designers typically need. In larger 3D programs such as Alias' Maya or Discreet's 3ds max, a lot of authoring time is spent deciding how objects will be textured, and a lot of render time is spent on how surfaces reflect each other. After Effects instead makes every surface a video file. This can be a faster and more intuitive approach to 3D for those with a video background.

Most 3D animation packages also have a 3D modeling program. In After Effects, modeling objects to use in your 3D composites is done in normal compositions. However, a few special steps are needed to incorporate them into the final animation, and any lights or cameras used in the model compositions are lost when the model comp is incorporated into an animation composition. (SEE FIGURE 07.)

Start by opening the project 2-Building *start.

Eventually this building will be used as a 3D model in our 3D city. Each building will need to look different. Each face of the building will be a duplicate copy of the building facade texture that we select for that building. In After Effects, it is the camera that is going to move around the buildings. The perspective of the camera to the building is what will angle and distort the building

COLLAPSE TRANSFORMATION

1. 3D model compositions are dragged into a main composition. This has the effect of collapsing all of the model parts (layers) into one 3D object in the main comp.

2. The Collapse Transformation switch must be turned on for the 3D model's layer in the main comp. Without it you will see only a picture of the 3D model in the main comp, rather than the actual model.

3. All lights and camera in the model's precomposition are disregarded. The only lights and cameras that affect the final render are the ones in the main composition.

faces to make it look three-dimensional. So we do not want our texture to look three-dimensional. The best texture is a flat texture or a straight-on view of the building.

These images were taken from stock photographs of buildings in Chicago. They were brought into Photoshop, trimmed down to rectangles, and desaturated to take out any color. Also, while in Photoshop it is sometimes helpful to note the size of the layers. Those numbers can come in handy later. This one is 134 pixels wide by 233 pixels high.

Next we want to duplicate the layer four times around a center point to make our rectangle into a 3D box. There are several ways to accomplish this, but I prefer to rotate around a layer's anchor point. If the edges of these building faces are to match up, and each is 134 pixels wide, then the center point of our box will be 67 pixels (134 divided by 2) behind the center of the current layer.

 ESSENTIAL KEYBOARD SHORTCUTS

S = Scale

P = Position

R = Rotation (and Orientation if the layer is 3D)

A = Anchor Point

T = Opacity

[= move layer's in-point to the time marker

] = move layer's out-point to the time marker

Cmd-D (Ctrl-D) = duplicate a layer

Cmd-G (Ctrl-G) = open the Go To Time box

Home and End = move time marker to beginning or end of the Timeline

J and K = move the time marker to next or previous visible keyframe

The main tools needed to effectively master 3D in After Effects are the Constrain Arrows and the 3D Views.

Using the Orbit Camera tool in a Custom View does not affect a composition. The position of layers and the way that the comp renders remain exactly the same. Orbiting the camera is simply a way to help you better understand where layers are positioned in 3D space.

For more detail on animating the building's entrance, go into the Project window, open the x-precomps folder, open the BLDGS folder, and double-click the Bldg 14 composition. This composition shows how masks were animated in the building precomps to add some movement to their entrance in the main comp.

08 » CONSTRAIN ARROWS USED IN 3D

1. Select the layer. Notice the Constrain Arrows at the anchor point. (SEE FIGURE 08.)

2. Set the third number of the anchor point (the Z-axis) to 67. This moves the anchor point of the layer 67 pixels (half the layer width) behind the layer.

3. Set your View to Custom View 1. (SEE FIGURE 09.)

4. Select the Orbit Camera tool. (SEE FIGURE 10.)

5. Click in the middle of the Display window and drag the cursor to the right. This will orbit the building face around to show the anchor point behind it.

6. Duplicate the Building Face layer. Select the Building Face 2 layer and set its Y-Rotation to 0x90.

7. Duplicate the layer again and set the new layer's Y-Rotation to 0x180.

8. Duplicate the layer again and set the new layer's Y-Rotation to 0x270. You should now have a building! (SEE FIGURE 11.)

9. Use the Orbit Camera tool to swoop around it and get a sense of how it will look from different camera angles.

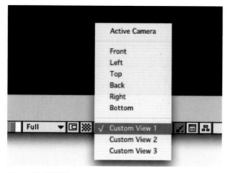

09 » 3D VIEWS

10 » ORBIT TOOL

11 » A SIMPLE 3D MODEL.

TYPING TIMECODE

When using the Go To Time box or setting the composition's duration, timecode does not need to be treated sensitively. Quickly typing a 300 will give you 3 seconds. Typing 1015 will give you 10 seconds and 15 frames. There is no need to take extra time to type in colons or semicolons.]

Tutorial 2 : Building the Skyline

"Smoke and mirrors" is my term for a type of trick that is constantly useful in After Effects. Many of the techniques used in the special effects field were invented by Alfred Hitchcock for films such as Vertigo. Hitchcock used smoke, mirrors, painted panes of glass, and projections to create the groundbreaking effects of his time. These days we have lots of fancy computers, yet often we use them to do the same things that Hitchcock did with his smoke and mirrors.

In this project, our smoke and mirrors refers to how we built the skyline. Rather than creating an entire city of buildings, we will create the illusion of an entire city of buildings. Once a few buildings have come into the scene, the audience has registered that they are looking at a city. They are sold on the effect, and from that point forward it is only a matter of maintaining that perception. Rather than trying to create hundreds of buildings for our city, we only create the first 10 and use a backdrop to give the illusion that these buildings continue into the distance.

1. Open the 3-Skyline *start composition. This is a duplicate of the final composition with the background layers turned off. Notice that even though there are 15 buildings in our city it still looks pretty sparse.(SEE FIGURE 12 & 13.)

2. Hold down the Option (Alt) key and double-click the Background New layer. This will take you into the Background New composition. (SEE FIGURE 14.)

12 » CITY WITH BACKDROP

13 » CITY WITHOUT BACKDROP

14 » BACKGROUND TAB

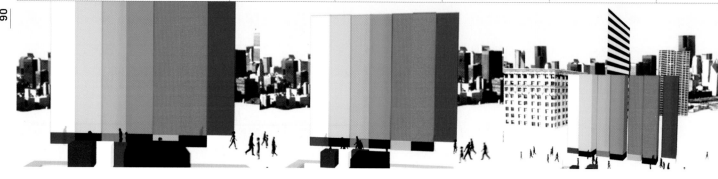

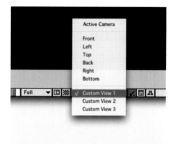

15 » TURN ON THE 3D SWITCH

16 » USE CUSTOM VIEW 1

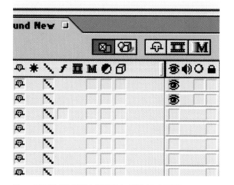

17 » TURN ON THE LAYERS A FEW AT A TIME

3. Turn on the 3D Switch for all the layers. (SEE FIGURE 15.) You can click on the first one, then while still holding the mouse button depressed, drag straight down to activate all layers.

4. Change the View menu in the Display window to Custom View 2. This allows us to select and use the Orbit Camera tool [009 Orbit Tool.tiff] to look around the composition in three dimensions, without altering the active camera or object layers' positions. (SEE FIGURE 16.)

5. At first, the Eyeball Switch on each layer is turned off. I like to start by assembling the source materials, then turning on the Eyeball Switch for a few layers at a time in order to assign them Positions and start times. Turn on the eyeball switch for the first two layers. (SEE FIGURE 17.)

6. These first two layers are base plates. They are designed to take up the majority of the city skyline area that the audience will see. Select the first layer and set its Scale to 1000.

7. Set the first layer's Position to –5522, –600, 2375, and its Orientation to 0, 270, 0.

Selecting a layer and pressing the ~ key will collapse it back to a single line in the Timeline. This helps to hide properties when you are done with them to keep the Timeline view concise.

8. Go To Time 116 and move the first layer's in-point to the time marker (use the [key). This layer is now posed to fill the left-hand view of the camera. (SEE FIGURE 18.)

9. Select the second layer and set its Position to 765, −415, 5515 and its Scale to 1750.

10. Go To Time 125 (the first time this layer will possibly be seen) and move the layers in-point to the time marker. (SEE FIGURES 19 & 20.)

11. Use the Orbit Camera tool to orbit around these two layers. Notice how their angle helps them to better fill the area.

12. Turn on the eyeball switch for Layers 3 and 4. These two layers have taller buildings which will sit behind the main backdrop layers to enhance the sense of depth in our skyline.

13. Select Layer 3 and set its Scale to 1100 and its Position to −2615, −990, −6070.

14. Select Layer 4 and set its Scale to 1700 and its Position to −1750, 1950, 7815.

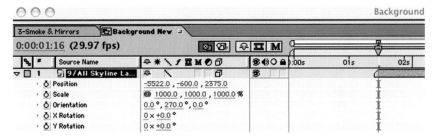

18 »

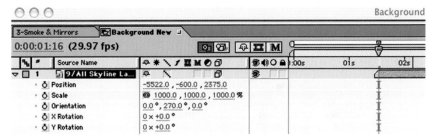

19 »

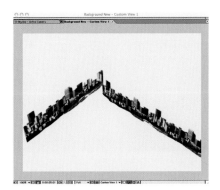

20 » DEPENDING ON HOW YOU USE THE ORBIT TOOL, YOU MAY HAVE A DIFFERENT VIEW THAN THIS.

21 »

PERSPECTIVE DISTORTION

As a 3D camera moves around a set of 3D layers, those at different depths will appear to move in relation to each other. Rotating a 2D photo in 3D space does not produce the same appearance. This effect is called perspective distortion, and it is how our eyes see depth in the physical world.

22 » TRUE 3D ROTATION WITH PERSPECTIVE DISTORTION REQUIRES THE COLLAPSE TRANSFORMATION SWITCH TO BE TURNED ON.

23 » ROTATING A FLAT 2D LAYER IN 3D SPACE. THERE IS NO PERSPECTIVE DISTORTION, AND COLLAPSE TRANSFORMATION IS TURNED OFF.ON.

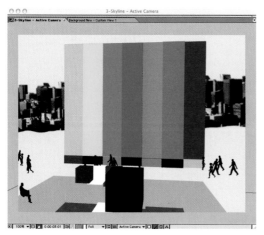

24 »

15. Use the Orbit Camera tool to orbit around the layers and get a sense of where they are positioned in relation to the first two backdrop layers. Layer 3 sits only slightly behind, while Layer 4 is positioned more than twice as far back. Layer 3 will have only a slight amount of perspective distortion compared to Layer 4. (SEE FIGURES 21, 22 & 23.)

16. When designing a composite of many objects, as is typically done in After Effects, you should be constantly concerned with how each object enters and exits the stage. When our camera pulls away from the color bars, the first two layers will be revealed on either sides of the color bar buildings. Go back to the 3-Skyline composition and Go To Time 3 seconds. (SEE FIGURE 24.)

17. Now Go To Time 400. At this point in our composition the town center is filled in with buildings. The backdrop is to a large extent visible between the main buildings, and thus this is a good time to start bringing in new buildings behind our main backdrop. Since these new elements are not the focus, a simple entrance is better than an attention-grabbing, effects-laden one. A simple fade-in will be more effective than anything else.

18. Hold down the Option (Alt) key and double-click the Background New layer. This will take you into the Background New composition and position the time marker at exactly the same point (4 seconds).

Background New • Timeline

| 3-Skyline | Background New | | | | | | | | |

0:00:05:00 (29.97 fps)

	#	Source Name										:00s	01s	02s	03s	04s	05s	06s
▷	1	9/All Skylin...															
▷	2	1/All Skylin...															
▽	3	10/All Skyli...															
	▷ Opacity	100%						✔									
▽	4	6/All Skylin...															
	▷ Opacity	100%						✔									

25 »

19. Select both Layers 3 and 4 and move their in-points to the time marker. Turn on the stopwatch for both of these layers' Opacity and set their Opacity to 0.

20. Go To Time 500 and set the Opacity of both layers to 100. (SEE FIGURE 25.)

21. Next we will add several more layers in different positions and at different depths to add more sophistication to the perspective distortion of the backdrop. Turn on the eyeball switch for Layers 5, 6 and 7.

22. Set Layer 5's Scale to 1900, its Position to –4570, –1300, 7350, and its Orientation to 0, 333, 0.

23. Set Layer 6's Scale to 1800, its Position to –13340, –20, –40, and its Orientation to 0, 280, 0.

24. Set Layer 7's Scale to 1700, its Position to –13300, –1690, 10425, and its Orientation to 0, 310, 0.

25. Set all three layers' in-points to 500, turn on the stopwatch for Opacity, and set each layer's Opacity to 0. Go To Time 515 and set the Opacity of all three layers up to 100. [024 layers567. tiff]

26. Use the Orbit Camera tool to orbit around the layers and get a sense of where they were positioned. Consider how the variation in depth and position will help to make the backdrop look more complex and convincing. (SEE FIGURES 26 & 27.)

27. Turn on the eyeball switch for Layers 8, 9, and 10.

26 »

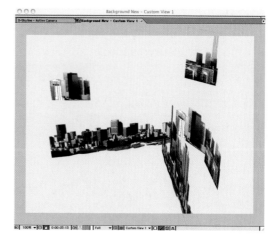

27 » PRACTICE WITH THE ORBIT TOOL BY TRYING TO MATCH THE ANGLE OF VIEW HERE.

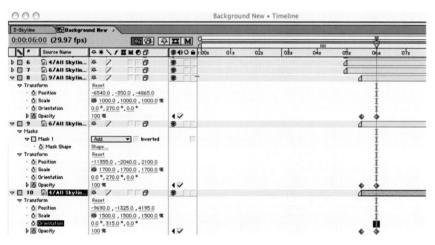

28 »

29 »

28. Set Layer 8's Scale to 1000, its Position to –6540, –350, –4865, and its Orientation to 0, 270, 0.

29. Set Layer 9's Scale to 1700, its Position to –11355, –2040, 2100, and its Orientation to 0, 270, 0.

30. Set Layer 10's Scale to 1500, its Position to –9690, –1325, 4195, and its Orientation to 0, 315, 0.

31. Set the in-point of Layers 8, 9, and 10 to time 515 and turn on their stopwatches for Opacity.

32. Set all three layers' Opacity to 0, Go To Time 600 and set it to 100. (SEE FIGURE 28.)

33. Use the Orbit Camera tool to orbit around the growing city backdrop. Layer 8 serves a slightly different purpose here than some of the previous layers. It extends the reach of the left side of our backdrop. When the camera move in the previous composition completes, the very left-hand edge of our skyline was showing. We want to keep the illusion that the skyline continues on in both directions, so a duplicate skyline piece has been placed just beyond the left edge to help this illusion. (SEE FIGURE 29.)

34. Each layer so far has been a group of buildings. Layers 11, 12, and 13 are single objects, which add just a few fi-

COMMERCIALS

Demo Reels

nal touches of variation and believability. Select Layers 11 and 12 and turn on their eyeball switches.

35. Set Layer 11's Scale to 160, Position to −2360, −755, −2455, and Orientation to 0, 270, 0.

36. Set Layer 12's Scale to 200, Position to −1260, −875, 4505, and leave Orientation at 0.

37. With the time marker at 600, set both layer's in-points to the current time, turn on the stopwatch for Opacity, and set Opacity to 0.

38. Go To Time 615 and set the Opacity of both layers to 100. (SEE FIGURE 30.)

39. Orbit around the objects in the Display window to see where their placement is. They were placed in front of the main backdrop to help bridge the viewer's eye from the 3D buildings to the flat photos of the backdrop. (SEE FIGURE 31.)

40. The final layer is a small airplane which flies across the sky.

41. Select Layer 13 and turn on its eyeball switch.

42. Go To Time 215 and set the layer's in-point to the current time.

43. Set the layer's Scale to 120 and its Orientation to 0, 77, 0.

44. Set its Position to −2840, −2280, 5410 and turn on the position stopwatch.

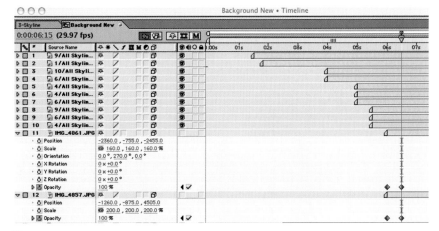

30 »

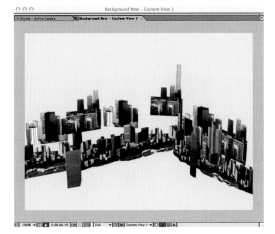

31 »

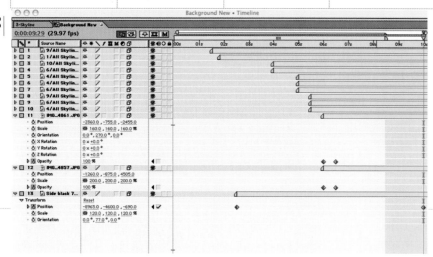

32 »

33 »

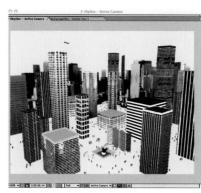

34 » STAGGER THE IN POINTS OF THE LAYERS

35 » TURN ON THE MOTION BLUR SWITCHES

36 »

45. Press the End key to go to the end of the Timeline, and set the layer's Position to –8965, –4600, –690. Scrub along the Timeline to watch the airplane's movement. (SEE FIGURE 32 & 33.)

46. One small way to add a bit of professionalism to this composite is to stagger the in-points of the layers. When groups of two or three layers are starting at the same time, pulling each of them forward or backward a few frames will help to make their entrance less synchronized and more spontaneous. (SEE FIGURE 34.)

47. Finally, turn on the Motion Blur switch for all the layers. Since 3D models use the Collapse Transformation switch, they rely on the Motion Blur of layers below. These layers in particular are not moving, but we want the camera movement around them to contribute to the motion blur. (SEE FIGURE 35.)

48. Use the tabs across the top of the Timeline to return to the 3-Skyline composition, and press the 0 key on the numeric keypad to do a RAM Preview. If you are not able to load the entire sequence into RAM, then reduce the composition's resolution down to Half and do another RAM Preview. (SEE FIGURE 36.)

37 »

Tutorial 3: Composition Timing

When the time for action comes, the time for preparation has passed. If you study how to operate a camera and shoot footage, the first and possibly most important lesson you would learn is that there is very little you can do once you get on location. The majority of hard work is done before you ever pick up a camera. This is called preproduction.

(SEE FIGURE 37 & 38.)

The importance of preproduction is just as true for video producers who use computers instead cameras. Every minute spent with a pen and paper saves 10 minutes of time in the program. Even the most adept After Effects user cannot create rough images in the program as fast as the imagination creates them in your mind.

(SEE FIGURE 39 & 40.)

38 »

39 »

40 »

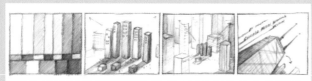

41 »

42 »

43 »

44 »

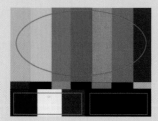

45 »

46 » THE COLOR RECTANGLES
ACROSS THE TOP AND MIDDLE
COME FROM THE COLORED
BUILDINGS, THE SQUARES IN
THE LOWER LEFT FROM THE
PARK BENCHES, AND THE

The best movies were labored over on paper, in Photoshop or in Illustrator. The individual scenes and transitions were visualized, considered, erased and redrawn, before the artist ever picked up a light pen or mouse. Begin with an idea and then figure out how to make the tools instantiate the vision; otherwise, the technology will entirely determine the tone and body of your message. **(SEE FIGURES 40-45.)**

With this project we began with the idea of a camera move which pulls away from color bars to reveal a 3D version of the city of Chicago. We knew that parts of the color bars needed to be comprised of actual 3D objects. **(SEE FIGURE 46.)**

So we conceived a series of buildings made of flat colors which would be the long stripes of color at the top of the color bar. We then considered a small park area which would have a tower and some benches that would form the bottom portion of the color bars.

Each of the color buildings and benches were constructed exactly as described in the previous tutorial. The buildings were positioned right next to each other, and that composition was placed in the scene in front of the camera's starting position.

1. **Open 1-Final Project.aep and go to Time Marker 2. Notice that even a full second after the camera move has begun, the color bars are still fully together.**

2. Select the BarsMain layer. It is right at this point that we want the buildings to start moving apart. Press the U key to reveal any keyframed parameters, and nothing happens. The building movement has been animated in the BarsMain precomp. But we need to see the camera move in this comp in order to know where to put the keyframes in the precomp.

3. Hold down the Option (Alt) key and double-click the BarsMain layer. The BarsMain precomp opens in your Display window, but the time marker is set at exactly the time corresponding to where the it was in the 1-FinalProject comp. Notice that each bar begins to move at this time.

4. Press the K key to move the time marker to the next keyframe at time 411. Click on the "1-Final Project" tab at the top of the Timeline window. (SEE FIGURE 47.)

5. Notice that the time marker is now at 411 and the Display window shows the color buildings after they have been moved apart.

Compositions and precompositions are two names for the same thing. The prefix indicates that the composition occurs before other compositions in the project flowchart. Not only does Option (Alt)+double-clicking a layer take you into the previous composition for that layer, but it also synchronizes the time between the two compositions. This allows you to place keyframes in previous compositions at exactly the right times for their action to correspond to the action in the main composition.

Also, the tabs across the top of the Timeline also become like a series of bread crumbs as you drill down through a chain of pre-

Holding down Option (Alt) and double-clicking a layer takes you into the pre-composition at exactly the equivalent point in the Timeline.

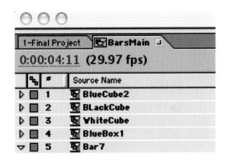

47 » TIMING IS SYNCHRONIZED BETWEEN COMPOSI-
    TIONS SHOWN IN TABS.

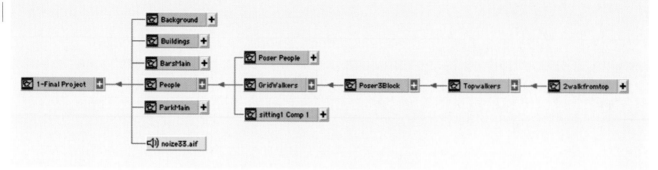

48 » FLOWCHART VIEW CAN BE A USEFUL TOOL TO UNDERSTAND COMPOSITION STRUCTURES.

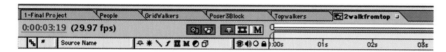

49 » THE TAB WELL CAN BE YOUR FRIEND.

50 » THE FLOWCHART BUTTON TAKES YOU INTO FLOWCHART VIEW.]

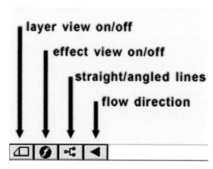

51 » FLOWCHART VIEW OPTIONS IN THE LOWER LEFT CORNER

compositions. Closing them as you move back up to the main composition helps to keep the Tab Well across the top of the Timeline window concise and understandable. **(SEE FIGURES 48 & 49.)**

Comp Flowchart View is provided within After Effects because flowcharts are a simpler way of depicting the variety of compositional structures that can be created inside the program. After Effects compositions can be combined in a more complex way than layers or sequences used in other programs like Photoshop or Final Cut Pro.

6. Open the 1-Final Project composition from the Project window and click the Comp Flowchart Button at the bottom-right side of the Display window. **(SEE FIGURE 50.)**

This launches the Comp Flowchart View. This is not an authoring part of the program; you cannot change the compositions from this window. The user interface is a bit hard to use, but with a little practice the Comp Flowchart View can become an essential part of both preproduction and project management. Holding down the spacebar gives you the Hand tool, which can be used to quickly navigate around a large flowchart. **(SEE FIGURE 51.)**

ABOUT THE ANIMATORS

Jason White, Daily Planet :: www.DailyPlanetLtd.com

Jason White began his art career drawing, painting, and studying the fine arts. An interest in digital art and animation led him to study 3D animation and motion graphics at the Illinois Institute of Art in Chicago. White currently works as Director of Motion Graphics at Daily Planet on a range of projects, including television shows, movie intros, commercials, and music videos. Daily Planet is a 25-year-old full-service editorial and motion graphics company located on the 29th floor of the NBC Tower in downtown Chicago. Clients include major advertising agencies, Dell, History Channel, and SC Johnson. Daily Planet Ltd. is an integral component to the thriving local post-production industry.

Nick Campbell, Creamy Orange :: www.CreamyOrange.com

Creamy Orange is the personal portfolio of Nick Campbell. The site has become a venue for his contemporary design techniques and multi-layered motion work. A self-proclaimed "Keyframe Scientist," Nick strives to become the first Motion Graphics Physicist, fusing intricate, subatomic details with strong nuclear ideas and gravitational design. Outside of the laboratory, you can usually find him with a camera in one hand and a cup of coffee in the other.

AUTHOR

Mason Dixon, Design After Next :: www.DesignAfterNext.com

Mason currently works as Chief Technology Officer of Design After Next, a thriving identity design firm. He is certified in video design and web media software by Apple, Adobe, and Macromedia. He studied at the Advanced Communications Technologies Laboratory in Austin Texas, and is a Nettime.org moderator. Current and past clients include the Navy Interactive Courseware Department, American Analog Set, Yahoo Chat, Mayo Clinic and DJ Spooky.

CHICAGO MOTION

The Chicago Motion Graphics Festival (CMGF) was founded out of a need to give the motion graphics artists and producers of the Midwest a forum for their cutting-edge creations. We are looking though a wide-angle lens at the motion graphics landscape, searching for the most innovative designs. We seek to promote those who are creating pioneering visuals, actively build an audience for Motion Graphics in the general public, and hope to inspire everyone else in the process.

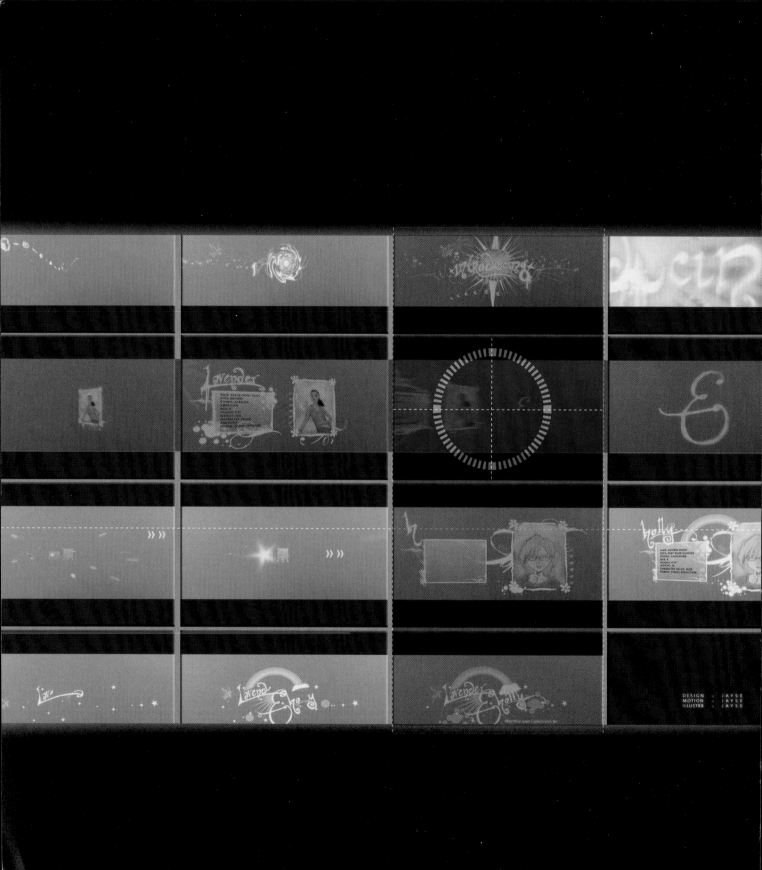

BUILDING A SHORT PROMO

JAYSE HANSEN

The story of Lavender & Holly (written and conceived by Kim Moore and Barbara Davis) needed a mock-up show intro to excite executives and investors and enable them to have a better taste of the women's unique vision for the show.

I used to design mock-up posters for Fox, CBS, and Fred Dryer Productions (of Hunter fame), and I always found them to be some of the most creatively freeing and challenging type of projects out there. Often, one person becomes the director, the designer and the animator. Expectations are not as high as they would be for broadcast work simply because the time allotted is scarce. However, since you usually get a lot more creative control, you might find yourself with an award-winning piece (such as I did with this one). If I haven't sold you on the benefits of doing this kind of work, I'll add that these clients also typically pay well—an added bonus, if you ask me.

WHAT'S ON THE DVD
:: Final Animation in QuickTime
:: Rough Camera Pass Quicktime
:: Various After Effects project files in 6.5 to illustrate techniques
:: Storyboard Template.doc

INTRODUCTION

Parameters

Watch the final animation on the DVD to see the end result. This piece began with the clients walking me through the character overviews and giving me a six-page treatment. It's easy to get overwhelmed when all the creative control is in your hands, so I usually begin by trying to find a single heart to the piece. I started asking the clients what they had in mind. It was obvious that they were passionate about the story and had clear ideas for their characters, but didn't have any artwork, logos, or visual ideas at all. They simply said, "Just make it very girly, with Mission Impossible-style stats for the girls; keep it high energy, and very cool."

My tasks became clear:

:: Come up with the logo, color scheme, look and feel of the project

:: Come up with rough sketches of the two main characters

:: Design and animate a short 30 to 40-second DVD intro that will motivate investors and publishers

:: Tie the menu to PDF and other interactive elements that would be saved on the DVD

:: Deliver everything in four days

⚙ **TOOLS USED**

:: **Laser Paper, Pencil and Gum Eraser (Storyboarding/Characters/Fonts)**

:: **Photoshop (Design Frames)**

:: **After Effects (Animation and Output)**

:: **Adobe Audition (Audio)**

Four days?

Four days is a bit less than I like to have for motion graphics pieces. Actually, I would have turned this job down since four days is really time only for research, a little design maybe, and not much more. The magic, the finesse, the genius is what gets lost on such short timelines. Unfortunately, that's what we sometimes have to deal with.

These clients were easy to work with and were fine with even a rough comp. They just needed something quick and were extremely appreciative. I found the project interesting and believed in it. So how could I refuse? I called my girlfriend, asked her for advice on what 'girly' meant to her and then told her I'd be home late.

The Design

I got started right away by researching some of the hottest "girly" things on the market. My first stop is typically images. google.com to start pulling together imagery to inspire the design. Second stop for this project was a toy store. Looking through various Barbie dolls, Bratz dolls and Fairy Houses, my main focus was: What colors are they using? What fonts? What type of look is popular?

If I'm unfamiliar with a subject, I like to saturate myself with it for a day or two by finding everything associated with it and compiling it all into one or more "inspiration boards" that I print out and hang on my wall.

In everything I saw one thing jumped out at me. Girls in today's culture are all about being proud to be unique. It's about attitude and style. I chose to reflect this in the piece.

After researching I sketched out some ideas for the characters, the composition, and the design of the piece.

Going by the character personality sheets my clients provided, I found that Holly was the shy-yet-happy little character, and Lavender was the one at the forefront with the attitude.

On the right are the designs roughed out for the characters' different personality traits. **(SEE FIGURES 01–03.)**

01-03 »

adventure

holly

HAIR: BROWN, SHORT
EYES: DEEP BLUE
SEX: FEMALE
CLOTHES: TOMBOY
SHOES: PUMAS
TRAITS: TALKATIVE
CHARACTER VALUE: JADE
POWER: CALMING

introducing

10-12 » THE DESIGN FRAMES ARE ALL ABOUT STYLE, ATTITUDE AND COMMUNICATION. JUST REMEMBER TO KEEP ALL YOUR LAYERS SEPARATE SO YOU CAN ANIMATE THEM IN AFTER EFFECTS.

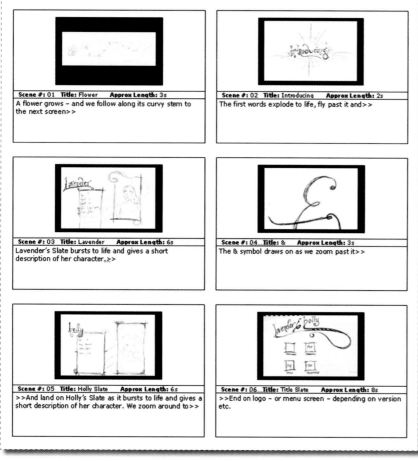

Scene #: 01 Title: Flower   Approx Length: 3s
A flower grows – and we follow along its curvy stem to the next screen>>

Scene #: 02 Title: Introducing   Approx Length: 2s
The first words explode to life, fly past it and >>

Scene #: 03 Title: Lavender   Approx Length: 6s
Lavender's Slate bursts to life and gives a short description of her character.>>

Scene #: 04 Title: &   Approx Length: 3s
The & symbol draws on as we zoom past it>>

Scene #: 05 Title: Holly Slate   Approx Length: 6s
>>And land on Holly's Slate as it bursts to life and gives a short description of her character. We zoom around to>>

Scene #: 06 Title: Title Slate   Approx Length: 8s
>>End on logo – or menu screen – depending on version etc.

Initial character roughs always help me get a better feel for the personality of the entire piece. These first sketches would help define the final designs: Lavender's design is bold and snappy with attitude while Holly's design is cute, positive and pretty.Next, I began working them into a simple storyboard format.

I decided on a camera fly-through type of look where the viewer would be introduced to the two characters, presented with a few quick stats (Mission Impossible – can't-read-it-all style), and then zoomed to the end card which would have their name and logo. Short and sweet. The storyboarding phase really helps to clarify it all. Even if you can't draw, I highly recommend using storyboards. I even used these in my initial camera path setup. **(SEE FIGURES 04–09.)**

So the next step is to scan these in and work up some design frames in Photoshop. **(SEE FIGURES 10-12.)**

04-09 » THERE'S NOTHING LIKE A FEW STORYBOARDS TO HELP A PIECE OUT. THIS IS WHERE YOUR FIRST EDITS SHOULD BEGIN. YOU SHOULD BE ALWAYS THINKING: "WHAT CAN I CUT?". A GOOD PIECE IS A PIECE THAT WOULD FALL APART IF ONE PART WERE REMOVED.

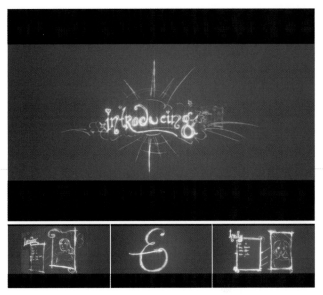

13-16 » THESE ARE THE SIMPLE PLACE HOLDERS I USED TO TWEAK MY CAMERA PATH.

The important thing when creating your design frames is to play as much as possible. Most of the greatest pieces of art, design, and motion graphics came as a result of the designer or artist exploring concepts. You can tell I made plenty of changes as the piece progressed, but the heart of it was always there.

For now, I just start putting stuff together. I then narrow it down to my favorites and present them to my clients. Luckily for me, they seemed to love these, and they got even more excited about the piece, which in turn, inspired me.

The Camera Path

Cameras in After Effects have always been frustrating. So are After Effects' velocity curves. People who don't find them frustrating are typically people who have never worked in other 3D packages and don't know what they're missing out on.

With this in mind, I plan my camera paths with stand-ins. The final designs will be animating and moving, but for planning my camera path I just need simple card placeholders so that I can focus on one thing: the camera.

For this I scanned in my storyboards, inverted them and added a pinkish-purple glow. For depth, the background is a simple gradient created in Photoshop. **(SEE FIGURES 13–16.)**

Straight camera paths are fairly straightforward (literally). Camera paths where you fly past a few cards going in a fairly straight line of motion don't require as much thought and tweaking. But I often prefer camera paths that turn and twist and spin and race, especially when I'm on such tight deadlines. I do seem to enjoy killing myself with so much extra work.

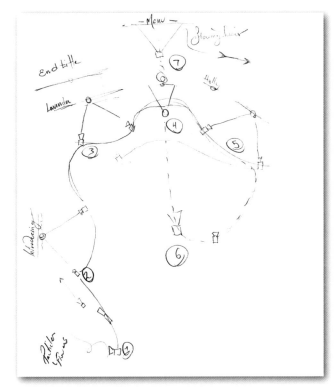

17 » THIS IS THE 'TOP DOWN' VIEW OF MY CAMERA PATH AND ALL THE SHOTS I WANT IT TO FOCUS ON. THIS HELPS A LOT WHEN WORKING WITHIN AFTER EFFECTS.

Tutorial

TO CREATE ADVANCED CAMERA PATHS:

:: Plan It

Start by drawing the path you want your camera to take, along with the camera's point of interest (what the camera is looking at) and the cards or screens that the camera will pass. The numbers in the drawing below correspond roughly to the

scene numbers on the storyboard. **(SEE FIGURE 17.)**

:: Set It Up

Next, create stand-in imagery of the same size and dimensions of your final designs. As I mentioned previously, I used simple storyboard drawings scanned in from my sketchbook. Switch to Top view (View>Switch 3D View>Top) in After Effects, zoom out and place these stand-

ins in roughly the same layout as your path-plan drawing. As you can see, mine follows my drawing pretty well, but I did make a few alterations. **(SEE FIGURE 18.)**

Here's how the camera path ended up in After Effects. It's pretty close to my drawing – with the main change at the end of the path where I decided a camera 'flip-around' would be a little more exciting than a dolly-type of push.

:: Create a Camera and a Null

You may have noticed that animating a camera inside After Effects can be quite a pain. This is typically because of the way you animate both the camera and the camera's point of interest. They often just don't do what you want them to.

I find it much easier to create a null object and attach the point of interest of the camera to it. This way you can animate the null and the camera independently, allowing for a better way of setting keyframes.

CREATE A CAMERA:

1. **Press Home to set your Timeline indicator to the beginning of your clip.**

2. **Ctrl-click (right-click) on a blank area in your Timeline and choose New>Camera, change settings if you want to, and click OK. I chose a 24mm camera, since I like the exaggerated perspective that wide-angle lenses can give.**

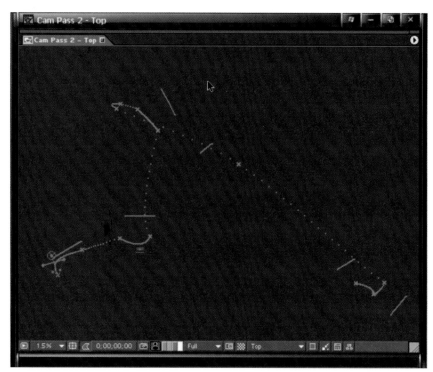

18 » HERE IS HOW THE CAMERA PATH TRANSLATES WITHIN AFTER EFFECTS. IT FOLLOWS THE PENCILED VERSION CLOSELY.

CREATE A NULL OBJECT:

1. Press Home to set your Timeline indicator to the beginning of your clip.

2. Ctrl-click (right-click) on a blank area in your Timeline and choose New>Null Object.

3. Click on the name of this new layer (Null1) and hit Return (Enter) to rename it. Name this new null object "POI" (point of interest) or something similar. Keep in mind however that what you name it will also be referenced in the expressions that are written in the following steps.

:: Next, parent the camera's POI to the null object.

1. Twirl down the triangle for POI's Transform function until you can see its Position property.

2. Also twirl down the triangle for your camera's Transform function until you see Point of Interest.

3. Option-click (Alt-click) the stopwatch related to the camera's Point of Interest function to set an expression for this property.

4. Immediately drag the pick whip related to the expression up to the Position property of the POI layer. This will write the expression: "thisComp.layer("POI").position." **(SEE FIGURE 19.)**

Now when you animate your POI null layer your camera's POI will follow along with it.

IMPORT THE SOUNDTRACK TO SYNC TO

This is a good time to bring in your music and start animating to it. To more accurately time the camera movements to the music, I first edited loops in Adobe Audition so that it was the right length for the clip I wanted to create. Then I brought the file in as a straight .wav file. (After Effects has problems rendering from MP3 files.)

:: Once you're in After Effects:

1. Drag the music file to your Timeline.

2. Make sure the audio layer is selected. RAM Preview the audio only using the period (.) key on your numeric keypad.

3. Mark each beat by pressing the * key on each beat as you listen to it. This will place markers on your layer, which you can then name (as shown in the following figure.) This also allows you to have a visual representation of the way the beats can affect the animation. **(SEE FIGURE 20.)**

19 » NOTICE THE EXPRESSION IS REFERENCING THE NULL OBJECT LAYER ABOVE IT. ANIMATING THE NULL IS THE BEST WAY OF ANIMATING YOUR CAMERA'S POINT OF INTEREST.

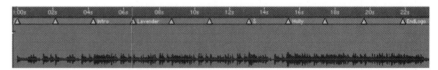

20 » THE TRIANGLES ON THE AUDIO LAYER ARE MARKS REPRESENTING THE MAJOR MUSIC BEATS. THE CAPTIONS INDICATE WHAT I WANT TO HAPPEN WHERE WITHIN THE MUSIC.

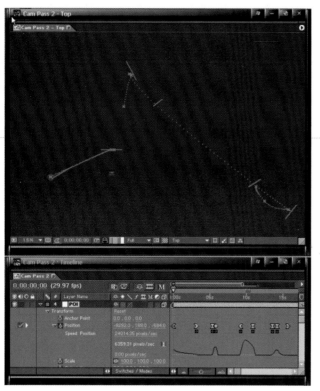

21 » TRY TO START SIMPLY BY ANIMATING ONE PROPERTY AT A TIME. THEN REFINE.

22 » ADDING VARIOUS PAINT SPLATTERS THAT I TAPED OUTSIDE HELPS TO ADD LIFE TO OTHERWISE STAGNANT OBJECTS.

CAMERA ANIMATION

Now animate your camera, one property at a time to keep it simple. For instance, animate the camera from the Top view first, and then animate the POI layer. After you're satisfied, switch to Camera view and tweak further. (SEE FIGURE 21.)

It pays to spend a lot of time getting your animation refined here before you start animating other elements (which will slow the rendering down.)

Making the Designs Come Alive

DRIPPING THINGS

Now on to the design part. (SEE FIGURE 22.)

For the various dripping, splattering elements, I got outside the box (meaning: the Computer) for a little bit and filmed them myself. I'll mention that you can also get a similar look by downloading the various dripping brush sets for Photoshop on the Adobe Exchange (studio.adobe.com) and animating masks to reveal them. But I'm an artist. I think it's a lot more fun to create this stuff myself. (And, of course, it's fun to see the more corporate types at your workplace walk by with puzzled expressions on their faces as you're tossing paint in front of your camera.)

:: To do this yourself:

Outside: Grab some white butcher paper or big poster board, set your camera up outside on a tripod and go to town with whatever runny paint you can get your hands on. I prefer black. The black on white will allow me to easily make it a track matte inside After Effects for whatever composite color or gradient I want to add to it. (SEE FIGURES 23–24.)

In After Effects: Capture it, bring it into After Effects, mask un-

The slicker the paper the better the paint will run. Get lots of it; you're building a stock collection here of organic stuff. You'll run out of paper fast. Water the paint down (if it's a water-based paint like tempera or similar) to make it more messy. Set your paper up as vertically as possible—stuff will drip better. You can always mask yourself and your paintbrush out later, but be mindful of getting yourself in the picture.

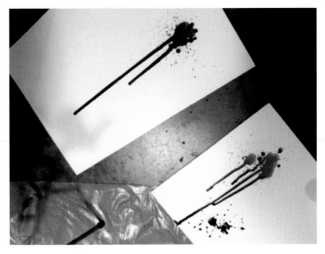

wanted stuff, and add Levels to heighten the contrast. Then add a new white layer above this, and make its track matte the luminance of the dripping footage. You've just created your own dripping stock footage with a perfectly clean straight alpha channel. Render this out with a straight alpha channel or as a 32bit PNG sequence, and you're set to use it wherever and however you want.

Optionally: If the neighbors don't mind, throw paint at your canvas. Splatters and streaks and all kinds of mess will find a home in some great motion graphics piece someday.

23 » RUNNY BLACK PAINT DRIPPED ONTO WHITE POSTER BOARD WAS FILMED WITH A STANDARD DV CAMERA TURNED ON ITS SIDE. THIS ALLOWS THE CAMERA TO 'FAKE' MORE RESOLUTION WHILE FILMING THE LONG DRIPS.

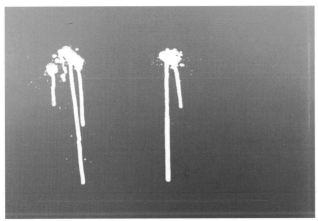

25 »

24 » IMPORTING THE FOOTAGE INTO AFTER EFFECTS, INVERTING IT AND CREATING A TRACK MATTE ALLOWS IT TO BE COMPOSITED OVER OTHER FOOTAGE.

HAIR: BROWN, SHORT
EYES: DEEP BLUE
SEX: FEMALE
CLOTHES: TOMBOY
SHOES: PUMAS
TRAITS: TALKATIVE
CHARACTER VALUE: JADE
POWER: CALMING

26 » OTHER ELEMENTS THAT APPEAR TO GROW ON ARE
VECTOR SHAPES WITH MASK PROPERTIES ANIMATED.

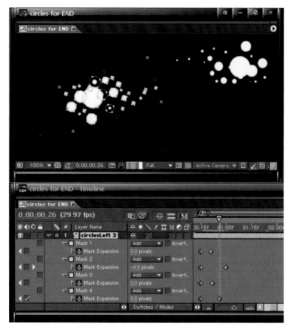

27 » ANIMATING THE MASK EXPANSION PROPERTY IS A SUPER-QUICK WAY
OF MAKING MASK SHAPES GROW-ON.

Growing Vector Flowers, Filigree, Ornaments and Other things

Other organic elements in the promo piece are simply vector shapes created in Photoshop, brought into After Effects as masks and animated. I often like to make things appear to grow or come alive. I've found it's a much better way to bring elements into a scene than simply motion-tweening or ramping their opacity. To find an extended video tutorial on this process, check out www. xeler8r.com. (SEE FIGURE 26.)

TO GROW YOUR OWN VECTOR PATHS:

1: Create numerous, randomly sized circles using the oval mask tool on a white solid inside After Effects.

2: Select all masks with the Shift key and twirl down to animate their mask expansion from a negative number back to their default setting of 100%.

3: Additionally, offset the keyframe sets for mask expansion randomly to get an organic growing effect. (SEE FIGURE 27.)

Optionally, to get a more bubbly or springy look, before you offset the keyframes, animate the mask expansion from a negative value to an overly positive value and then back to 100%. This makes the animation come alive by springing the animation into its final state, rather than just a straight small-to-final type of look. **(SEE FIGURE 29.)**

Gotcha! I've found that if you do this technique to too many masks on one layer (30 circle masks, for instance) you may get an "Advanced 3D Render error" when rendering out this with a complex comp. To avoid this while working, don't use the Open GL preview features when working with multiple masks expansions. Use Adaptive Resolution instead.

Another easy fix is to make a proxy which you'll use in the final render. To do this:

1: **Ctrl click (Right click on the comp in the Project window and select Create Proxy>Movie.**
2: **In the Render Queue, change to Best Settings and the output to render as Quick Time with PNG compression set to Millions of Colors+ (to include the alpha channel), (Format Options>Compressor>PNG Depth>Millions of Colors +)**
3: **When you do your final render just make sure 'Current Settings' is selected from the dropdown in the "Use Proxies" setting of the Render Queue to avoid using the buggy source layer.**

28 » **MAKE SURE YOU'RE PREVIEWING WITH ADAPTIVE RESOLUTION TO AVOID RENDER ERRORS.**

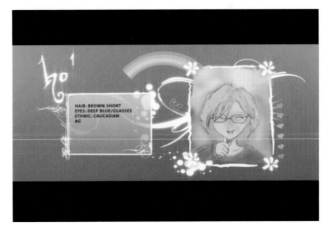

29 »

30 »

The Handwritten Effect

There are lots of elements in this piece that appear to be handwritten. For this work I created my graphics with a pencil on real paper and scanned them in. Sure, there are plenty of handwritten fonts you can buy, but those are other people's scribbles. Why not scribble your own masterpiece? **(SEE FIGURE 30.)**

Regardless of whether you've scanned your art in or you're using a font, the process is roughly as follows:

1. **Import your artwork. In this example – it's my scribbles, inverted in Photoshop so that they appear white.**

2. **In After Effects, select the layer and type Cmd Shift C (Ctrl Shift C) to Pre-comp the artwork. (Select Move all attributes to the new composition and deselect 'Open New Composition') You do this because you need the artwork to have the same pixel dimensions as your Comp for this trick to work.**

3. **Use the Pen tool to trace over it. Add as few points as possible, and add them in the order that you would draw the piece on.**

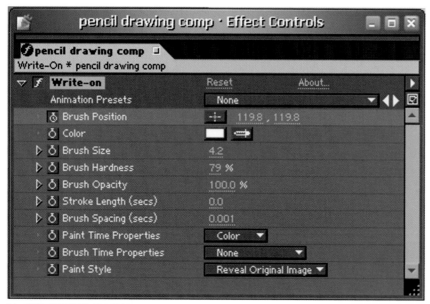

31 » USING THE WRITE ON EFFECT IS ANYTHING BUT SELF-EXPLANATORY. ONCE YOU GET IT, HOWEVER, IT BECOMES A POWERFUL ADDITION TO YOUR AFTER EFFECTS ARSENAL.

4. Choose Effect>Stylize>Write-on and set its Paint Style function to Reveal Original Image. **(SEE FIGURE 31.)**

5. Select the Pre-comped layer, press M, and select the Mask Shape property.

6. Press Cmd-C (Ctrl-C) to copy.

7. Type 'e' to reveal your effects and twirl down the Write-on function and select the Brush Position property.

8. Press Cmd-V (Ctrl-V) to paste the mask position as keyframes.

9. Play the animation to see it draw on. You may need to increase the brush size to see it.

10. Increase the brush size until it covers your artwork.

11. Decrease the brush spacing to .001.

12. Drag the end keyframe to slow the animation or speed it up. You'll notice that the inner keyframes are pasted as roving keyframes so they'll adapt automatically. **(SEE FIGURE 32.)**

32 » NOTICE THAT EACH BEZIER POINT IN YOUR MASK HAS BEEN PASTED AS A KEYFRAME. THE MIDDLE KEYFRAMES ARE ROVING, ALLOWING YOU TO SELECT THE BEGINNING OR END KEYFRAME AND EASILY DRAG TO SPEED-UP OR SLOW-DOWN THE ANIMATION.

Delivery

The final project had a unique, positive, girlish look, custom fonts, a custom logo, character development, character sketches and a final animation—all within a crazy short deadline. The clients were more than pleased, and I had a fun time doing it. Which is, after all, the point, isn't it? I hope this case study helps you with your own projects.

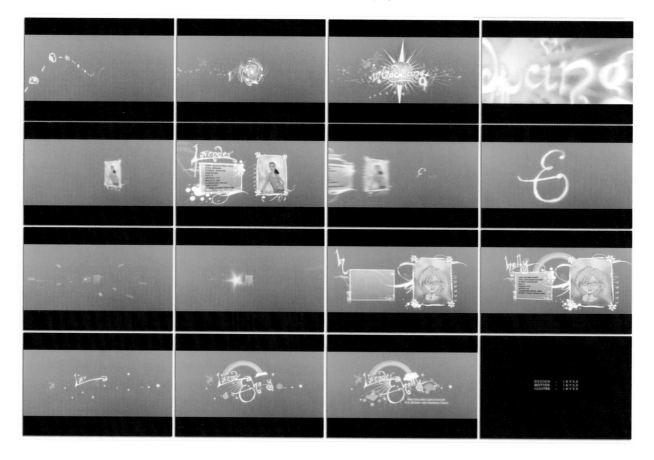

ABOUT THE AUTHOR

Jayse Hansen is Creative Art-Director for SMG in Las Vegas. In addition to designing print, web, and motion graphics for national clients such as Coca-Cola, MTV, HBO, and CBS, he has been featured in numerous books and articles on design and fine art. His motion art has been commissioned by night clubs and restaurants such as The Hard Rock Café and by luminaries such as Donald Trump. Recently he began sharing his knowledge and passion for good design through classes and video training on the high-end design portal called Xeler8r: www.xeler8r.com. You can also find him as a forum leader at www.creativecow.net. You can reach him at cmp@jayse.us.

FURTHER READING

Type in Motion
Matt Woolman
(Rizzoli 2001)

Non-Designer's Type Book
Robin Williams
(Peachpit 1998)

WEBSITES

xeler8r.com

creativecow.com

mograph.net

THE COLORIST'S TOOLBOX

MARIANNE POST

This chapter delves into the colorist and online editor's toolbox and provides a comprehensive color correction resource guide.

After Effects may not be the first application that comes to mind for color correction. Actually, certain color and luminance considerations should always be weighed when compositing such elements as text, glows, and imported video. While hanging out in After Effects, why not take advantage of its color-correction resources? This chapter delves into the colorist and online editor's toolbox and provides a comprehensive resource guide. So, roll up your sleeves, because you're going to sort through the tools that will help you make better color decisions and build confidence in using After Effects filters such as the Shadow/ Highlight effect (version 6.5 or later), Synthetic Aperture's Color Finesse plug-in (bundled with 6.5 pro),and many more.

WHAT'S ON THE DVD
Included on the DVD are source files and corrected color files.

INTRODUCTION

Video Levels Checklist

Most non-linear editing (NLE) systems offer corrective tools and broadcast filters that can compensate for color selections made in After Effects. However, these tools combined with poor color-correction decisions can distort or compromise the quality of a composite. To avoid this, keep the following considerations in mind:

1. Be consistent. For example, some NLEs allow RGB or 601 color mapping for export and import. If the image is exported at 601 levels, re-import the final artwork at 601 levels.

2. Select video-safe luminance and chrominance for borders, gradients, and glows. This means each channel should fall between 16 and 235. And remember that red bleeds on TV.

3. Color effects influence luminance levels.

4. Perform a test render to play back in the NLE, but make necessary adjustments in After Effects.

5. Crop out vertical and horizontal blanking that falls within the action-safe area.

6. Monitor images through an external broadcast display. Computer monitors display luminance and chrominance information differently than a video display does.

7. Check levels in a waveform monitor and vectorscope. Designated hardware scopes work best because of their high resolution and real-time feedback, but software scopes work better than nothing. Synthetic Aperture's Color Finesse, which is bundled with After Effects 6.5 Pro, is equipped with software scopes.

8. Monitor the levels for backgrounds created in After Effects or imported from third-party suppliers. Keeping levels between 16 and 235 is a good rule of thumb.

9. Be sure still images are prepared with the appropriate pixel aspect ratio.

TIP // In the Output Module of the Render Settings dialog box, do not vertically stretch images. Interlacing will compromise vertical resolution.

» REPRESENTS A PERFECT CIRCLE CREATED WITH THE INCORRECT SQUARE PIXEL FRAME SIZE SETTING IN PHOTOSHOP

» REPRESENTS A PERFECT CIRCLE CREATED WITH THE CORRECT SQUARE PIXEL FRAME SIZE SETTING IN PHOTOSHOP

10. Keep this checklist in mind when creating composites for high-definition projects. Most likely the program will be aired in standard definition as well

Pixel Aspect Ratio

To avoid image distortion, use **TABLE 1** as a guide for determining frame size settings.

Color Space

Non-linear editing (NLE) systems typically capture video with either RGB or ITU-R BT.601 color levels. Consistency is key when moving images between After Effects and the NLE. RGB deals in absolute values without headroom. Black is mapped to 0 and white is mapped to 255. Levels that fall below 0 and above 255 are clipped and cause loss of detail in shadows and highlights. Banding and other distortion may also result. The 601 color space allows for headroom. Black is mapped to 16 and white is mapped to 235. Because of this headroom and foot room, levels that fall between 0 and 16 (superblack) or between 235 and 255 (superwhite) have more give and won't lose detail. After Effects works in the RGB color space natively. The following table compares RGB and 601 mapping. **(SEE TABLE 2 & 3.)**

Color Correction Workspace

Proper setup will make the color-correction process easier. Here are the hardware and setup considerations:

1. **Properly calibrated broadcast video display**

2. **External waveform monitor and vector scope for monitoring the luminance and chrominance**

3. **For best results perform color correction in a room with neutral lighting (6500 degrees Kelvin) and a neutral gray backdrop placed behind the video display**

Format	4:3 Square Pixel Aspect Ratio	16:9 Square Aspect Ratio	Non-Square Pixel (After Effects and NLEs)
NTSC	648x486 720x540	864x486	720x486
NTSC DV	640x480 720x534	853x480	720x480
PAL	768x576	1050x576	720x576
HDTV 720p 16:9		1280x720	960x720
HDTV 1080i 16:9		1920x1080	1280x1080

TABLE 1

	RGB	Composite (IRE)	PAL and Component (mV)
Video black	0	7.5	0
Video white	255	100	700

TABLE 2 » RGB COLOR SPACE

	RGB	Composite (IRE)	PAL and Component (mV)
Video black	16	7.5	0
Video white	235	100	700
Superblack	0	0.74	−51
Superwhite	255	108.4	763

TABLE 3 » ITU-R BT.601

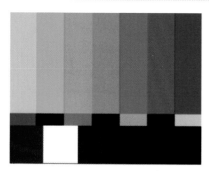

01 » SMPTE COLOR BARS

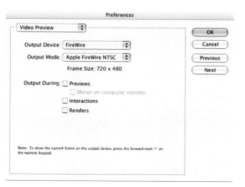

02 » PREVIEW PREFERENCES

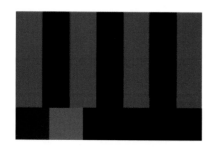

03 » BLUE ONLY MODE. IF THE MONITOR DOESN'T HAVE A BLUE ONLY MODE, PLACE A WRATTEN #47B FILTER IN FRONT OF THE MONITOR. THIS CAN BE PURCHASED AT A PHOTO SUPPLY STORE.

Tutorial 1:

Video Display Connection and Calibration

After Effects 6.5 can send a preview to an external video display. This tutorial walks through the video display connection and calibration workflow.

1. Connect the video display.

2. Open the ColorCorrect project on the DVD.

3. Load the 01_Monitor Calibration composition in the Tutorials folder. The composition contains SMPTE color bars. (SEE FIGURE 01.)

4. Select Video Preview from the After Effects menu (the Edit menu in Windows). (SEE FIGURE 02.)

The preferences have already been set for this project, but let's take a closer look at the preference options.

Output Device: Selects how the device is connected to the computer.

Output Mode: The options displayed here depend on the Output Device setting. The resulting frame size and frame rate appear below the selection.

Output During: Sets which operations are sent to the video display, such as RAM previews and scrubbing.

The video monitor should be calibrated to

ensure accurate display.

1. Press / (forward slash) to display the Timeline's current frame on the video monitor.

2. Adjust the brightness control on the video display until the left two bars of the pluge pattern aren't visible and the right-most strip is barely visible. (The pluge pattern is the set of three vertical strips at the lower-right portion of the monitor below the red color bar.)

3. Adjust the video display's contrast until the white square (to the left of the pluge pattern) looks white, not gray, and doesn't bleed over into the two neighboring color squares.

4. Enable Blue Only mode on the external monitor. (SEE FIGURE 03.)

5. Adjust the hue control (which may be labeled "tint" or "phase") until the upper and lower strips of the middle blue bar look the same.

6. Adjust the chroma (saturation) until the upper and lower strips of the two outer blue bars look the same.

7. Hue and saturation adjustments affect each other, so additional hue adjustments may be necessary. Calibration is finished, when both hue and chroma (saturation) are even.

8. Turn off Blue Only mode.

:: VIDEO SCOPES

Because the waveform monitor and vec-

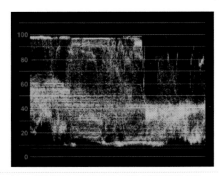

04 » SYNTHETIC APERTURE'S LUMA WAVEFORM. THE SCOPE UPDATES IN REAL TIME AS ADJUSTMENTS ARE MADE.

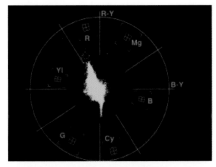

05 » SYNTHETIC APERTURE'S VECTORSCOPE

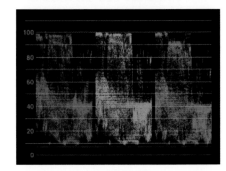

06 » APERTURE'S RGB WAVEFORME

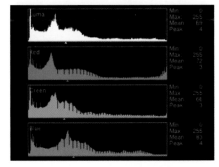

07 » SYNTHETIC APERTURE'S VECTORSCOPE

TIP // Check capture card documentation for Color space specifications.

---

torscope are integral to the color-correction toolbox, it's important to understand how they work. Following is a rundown of commonly used video scopes.

Waveform monitor: Measures a clip's luminance or brightness. This scope is useful when making tonal range adjustments, that is, setup (black levels), gain (white levels), and gamma (midtones). Lower levels, like shadows, appear near the bottom of the waveform display and brighter levels, like highlights, appear near the top of the display. **(SEE FIGURE 04.)**

Vectorscope: Measures a clip's hue and saturation. Hue is measured as an angle around the circle of the scope. The distance from the center of the scope measures saturation. This scope is useful for adjusting skin tone and neutralizing color casts.**(SEE FIGURE 05.)**

RGB parade: A commonly used software scope that measures the brightness for each of the red, blue, and green components separately. This scope helps identify color casts. Shadow information for each color appears near the bottom of the display and Highlight information appears near the top. **(SEE FIGURE 06.)**

Histogram: Another commonly used software scope that functions similarly to the level's histogram in After Effects. This scope shows distribution of pixels. The horizontal graph displays luma values, and the vertical display shows the portion of the images pixels present for each luma level. **(SEE FIGURE 07.)**

:: ANALYZING FOOTAGE

Before applying color-correction to an image or adding color to a composite there are several criteria to consider. The following checklist can help with analysis:

1. Unless a special treatment is applied, images should have a black point and a white point.

2. An image should have evenly distributed luminance levels and not be heavily weighted toward the darks or lights. A washed-out, flat-looking image can be greatly enhanced by opening up its tonal range.

3. Texture is key. An image should have detail in its darkest and lightest regions.

4. Flesh tones should be accurate.

5. Color casts should be neutralized, meaning that blacks should be black, not reddish or blueish, and whites should be white.

6. Sampling regions with a color picker can help pinpoint luma and chroma issues.

08 » WORKING IN 8-BIT MODE SPEEDS UP THE EFFECT DESIGN PROCESS. DURING OU PUT BE SURE TO SET BIT DEPTH TO 16-BIT MODE.

TIP // For the artist who's compositing with the standard version of After Effects and doesn't have access to external scopes, there's another software solution. Check out www. metadma.com for more information.

:: WORKFLOW

The final assets found in a colorist's toolbox are proper workflow and experience. The color-correction process becomes easier with each project. Here's a recipe for successful workflow:

Stage 1: Enhance an image's tonal range (luminance or brightness and contrast adjustments).

1. Set the black point.
2. Set the white point.
3. Set the gamma (gray point or balance of black to white).

Stage 2: Neutralize color casts such as white-balance issues or blue video.

1. Neutralize the blacks or shadow regions.
2. Neutralize the whites or highlights.
3. Neutralize the midtones or gamma.
4. Adjust inaccurate flesh tones (gamma adjustment).

Stage 3: Ensure shot-to-shot consistency (comparing shots with adjacent shots or blue video).

1. Select a clip or element from within the composite that is to serve as a reference shot or benchmark for matching other elements or adjacent shots.
2. Adjust other elements or adjacent shots to match or blend with this reference. A separate effect or adjustment layer can be introduced to separate this stage from stages 1 and 2.

Stage 4: Adjust the final look or style.

1. Apply an effect to an individual layer or adjustment layer and generate a stylized look.
2. Isolate a specific region and apply a secondary or spot correc-

tion effect or mask. For example create a photographer's color grad filter by isolating a washed out sky.

Stage 5: Check broadcast levels.

1. Manually check the levels of the composite in video scopes and make adjustments.
2. Apply a broadcast color filter or utilize Color Finesse's Level Limiting tool.

:: STANDARD EFFECTS

The remaining sections of this chapter implement this recipe. This section highlights useful manual color correction effects found under Effect>Adjust. The effects not covered in this section tend to introduce undesirable artifacting or have been made obsolete by an effect covered here. Because Auto filters can behave unpredictably, they will be covered after exploring how to work with manual effects. Some filters achieve the same results through different techniques. Determining which effect to add to the color-correction toolbox is largely a personal preference.

:: 16-BIT VERSUS 8-BIT:

High-resolution footage and high-definition (HD) footage will benefit from After Effect's 16-bit-color mode. This mode opens up a wider color range and enhances the quality of narrow color ranges (gradients). Most operations in After Effects can be executed in 16-bit mode. A yellow warning symbol appears next to an effect in the Effect Controls window that doesn't support 16-bit mode. Switch the setting back to 8-bit for these effects or details will be lost.

:: TO SETUP FOR 16-BIT DEPTH:

1. Choose File>Project Settings.

TIP // Tonal range should be adjusted first, even when facing blatant color casts like white-balance issues.

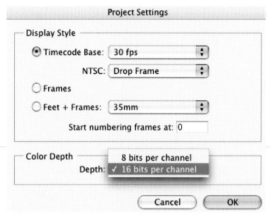

09 » PROJECT SETTINGS

2. Select "16 bits per channel" from the Color Depth pop-up menu.

3. To toggle between color depths, Opt-click (Alt-click) on the color depth indicator at the bottom of the Project window. **(SEE FIGURES 08 & 09.)**

:: LEVELS AND LEVELS (INDIVIDUAL CONTROLS)

These effects adjust a clip's tonal range and hue offsets and is the most commonly used standard effect. It includes a histogram that displays brightness levels for each pixel in an image. This effect quickly adjusts for low or flat contrast and can neutralize a color cast. Levels (Individual Controls) displays each channel in a list and allows individual keyframing.

1. Launch After Effects and open the ColorCorrect project if it's not currently open.

2. Load the 02_Levels composition, located in the Tutorials folder. Let's adjust the tonal range and remove the color cast for ExteriorCU.mov.

3. In the Timeline window, select the ExteriorCU.mov layer, and choose Effect>Adjust>Levels.

4. With RGB selected in the Channel property, drag the Input Black triangle to the right, drag the Input White triangle to the left, and adjust the Gamma triangle to taste.

5. Select Green from the pop-up menu in the Channel property.

6. Drag the Green Input Black triangle to the right, drag the Green Output White triangle to the left, and drag the Green Gamma triangle to the right.

7. Select Blue from the pop-up menu in the Channel property, drag the Blue Output Black triangle to the right, and drag the Blue Input White triangle to the left.

8. Select Red from the pop-up menu in the Channel property.

10 » INITIAL LEVELS

11 » ADJUSTED LEVELS

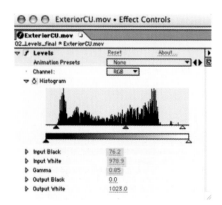

12 » LEVELS EFFECT ADJUSTMENTS MADE TO EXTERI-ORCU.MOV

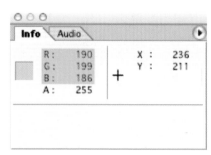

13 » LOOK AT THE INFO WINDOW (WINDOW>INFO) TO MONITOR RGB LEVELS.

14 » CURVES ADJUSTMENT APPLIED TO LEISURE2. MOV. ALTHOUGH KEYFRAMES CAN BE ADDED, IT'S NOT RECOMMENDED BECAUSE UNDESIR-ABLE ARTIFACTS MAY BE INTRODUCED.

9. Drag the Red Input Black triangle to the right, and drag the Red Gamma triangle to the left.

10. Select RGB from the pop-up menu in the Channel property and adjust the black, white, and gamma points.

11. To see a final correction, refer to the 02_Levels_final composition located in the Final folder.

12. Color-correct the Exterior_still.tif image in the 02_Levels composition. Use the 02_Levels_final composition as a reference. (SEE FIGURES 12 & 13.)

:: CURVES

The Curves effect makes adjustments similar to Levels, but instead of being limited to three slider controls, the Curves graph can handle up to 16 control points. These points isolate an adjustment to a more narrow range of values. The lower-left portion of the graph adjusts dark levels. The upper-right portion adjusts white levels. With practice, you can use this effect in very powerful ways, especially when correcting images with too much contrast.

1. Load the 03_Curves composition, located in the Tutorials folder.

2. In the Timeline window, select the Sunset.mov layer.

3. Choose Effect>Adjust>Curves.

4. With RGB chosen in the pop-up menu in the Curves property, raise the black point slightly and lower the white point slightly.

5. Click and drag midway down the line to add a control point and adjust the midtones.

6. Select Red from the Channel pop-up menu and add control points to adjust the hue. If necessary, click and drag a control point off the graph to delete it.

7. Select Blue from the Channel pop-up menu. Click and drag a midpoint control point to adjust the hue.

8. To see a final correction, refer to the 03_Curves_final composition located in the Final folder.

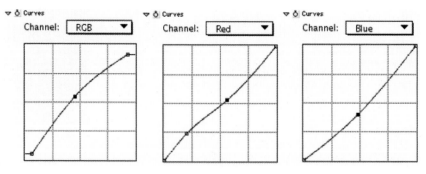

TIP // To avoid undesirable levels adjustments, leave Preserve Luminosity checked.

9. For additional practice, color-correct leisure2.mov in the 03_ Curves composition. Use the 03_Curves_final composition as a reference. **(SEE FIGURE 14.)**

:: HUE/SATURATION AND COLOR BALANCE

This effect modifies the hue, saturation, and lightness of a specified color range within an image. By checking the Colorize checkbox, this effect transforms into a tint effect. Similarly, the Color Balance effect has a simple interface for adjusting the amount of red, green, and blue. It can isolate just shadows, midtones, or highlights separately. Both effects easily adjust background textures and simple color elements.

1. Load the 04_HueSaturation composition located in the Tutorials folder. Background1.mov is over saturated.

2. Apply the Hue/Saturation effect to background1.mov.

3. Select Reds from the Channel Control pop-up menu.

4. Drag the two squares in the middle closer together to narrow the adjustment range. Drag the triangles closer together to lower feathering.

16 » AFTER THE CURVE ADJUSTMENT.

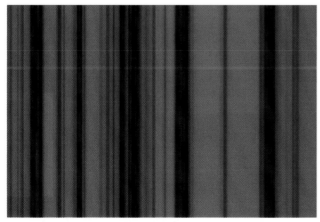

17 » BEFORE THE HUE/SATURATION ADJUSTMENT.

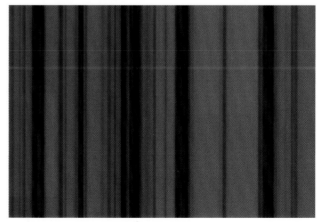

18 » AFTER THE HUE/SATURATION ADJUSTMENT.

19 » HUE/SATURATION EFFECT APPLIED TO BACKGROUND1. MOV

20 » PHOTO FILTER APPLIED TO THE EXTCU_CORRECT LAYER

21 » BEFORE THE PHOTO FILTER EFFECT.

22 » AFTER THE PHOTO FILTER EFFECT

5. Lower the red saturation by dragging the Red Saturation slider to the left.

6. Select Blues from the Channel Control pop-up menu. Lower the saturation and raise the lightness.

7. Select Magentas from the Channel Control pop-up menu and drag the Magenta Saturation slider to the left slightly.

8. Refer to 04_HueSaturation_final to see a final correction.

9. For additional practice, add the Hue/Saturation effect to background2.mov in the 04_HueSaturation composition. Use the 04_HueSaturation_final composition as a reference. (SEE FIGURE 19.)

:: PHOTO FILTER EFFECT

Introduced in version 6.5, this effect simulates a tinted filter being placed in front of a camera's lens for color style and balance purposes. The Photo Filter effect's Filter menu contains a variety of hue presets. It's possible to choose a custom color, too. The Density slider controls the amount of change.

1. Load the 05_PhotoFilter composition located in the Tutorials folder. This composition contains the clips corrected in the Levels tutorial. The photo filter effect can warm up the ExtCU_correct layer's color temperature.

2. Select the ExtCU_correct layer and choose Effect>Photo Filter.

3. Select Warming Filter (81) from the Filter pop-up menu and adjust the density to taste.

4. Refer to the 05_PhotoFilter_final composition to view a final correction.

5. Experiment with additional filters and densities. For additional practice, apply the Photo Filter effect to the Ext_still_correct layer. (SEE FIGURE 20.)

23 » THE SHADOW/HIGHLIGHT FILTER RESCUES SANTIAGO2.TIF.

:: SHADOW/HIGHLIGHT

This effect is a strong addition to version 6.5, and goes beyond the controls of Levels because it lightens and darkens regions based on surrounding pixel values. The default settings automatically adjust poorly backlit footage. The manual controls bring back detail lost in dark and light regions.

1. Load the 06_ShadowHighlight composition, located in the Tutorials folder.

2. In the Timeline, select the Santiago2.tif layer. The Shadow/Highlight effect can bring back the lost details of the mountains and enhance the texture of the trees.

3. Choose Effect>Adjust>Shadow/Highlight.

4. Deselect the Auto Amounts checkbox.

5. Lower Shadow Amount to about 30.

6. Raise Highlight Amount to about 80.

7. Click the More Options triangle.

8. Increase the Highlight Tonal Width, Highlight Radius, and Midtone Contrast to bring out the detail of the mountains without introducing undesirable artifacts.

9. Refer to 06_ShadowHighlight_final to see a final correction.

10. For additional practice, add the Shadow/Highlight effect to volcano1.tif in the 06_ShadowHighlight composition. Use the 06_ShadowHighlight_final composition as a reference. (SEE FIGURE 23.)

24 » BEFORE THE SHADOW/HIGHLIGHT EFFECT.

25 » AFTER THE SHADOW/HIGHLIGHT EFFECT.

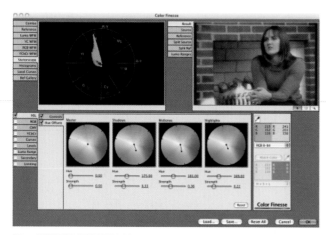

26 » SYNTHETIC APERTURE'S COLOR FINESSE USER INTERFACE. WARNING: THIS IS A POWERFUL PLUG-IN, SO REFER TO THE MANUAL FOR FURTHER GUIDANCE.

:: PRO EFFECTS

The Pro edition of After Effects includes two additional corrective filters: Color Stabilizer (bundled) and Color Finesse (separate installation). Go to www.synthetic-ap.com to download a demo version of Color Finesse to try out in the standard edition of After Effects.

:: Color Finesse

Color-correction between tabs in Color Finesse is cumulative, and each parameter is processed in a specific order. Although the tutorials in this chapter use just one tab at a time, many corrections will incorporate multiple tabs. **(SEE FIGURE 26.)**

Here's the processing order:

1. Levels pane, Input section

2. HSL pane, Controls pane, Master pane, Highlights pane, Midtones pane, Shadows pane

3. HSL pane, Hue Offsets pane

4. Curves pane

5. Levels pane, output section

6. Secondary pane

7. Limiting pane

[Note: Color Finesse uses a 32-bit floating-point color space, producing higher-quality output than 8-bit or 16-bit color spaces.]

:: SETUP

The color space of the source video's NLE determines Color Finesse's preference setup. The settings should match the source video's color space (RGB or 601). To apply Color Finesse and set the preferences:

27 » INITIAL COLOR FINESSE

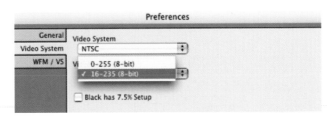

28 » COLOR FINESSE PREFERENCES. THE VIDEO CODING SETTINGS AFFECT HOW IMAGES APPEAR IN THE VIDEO SCOPES LOCATED IN THE ANALYSIS WINDOW.

1. Select a layer, and choose Effect>Synthetic Aperture>SA Color Finesse.

2. Click the Setup button in the Effect Controls window. This launches the user interface (UI).

3. Choose SA Color Finesse UI>Preferences.

4. Activate the Video System tab. Set Video Coding levels to match color space of source footage.

5. If necessary, check the "Black has 7.5% Setup" checkbox.

6. Click OK. **(SEE FIGURE 28.)**

   [Note: If the source footage was captured with a RGB codec, set Processing to 0–255. If footage captured with 601 color levels, for example, Avid QT codec, set Processing to 16–235.] **(SEE FIGURE 29.)**

29 » COLOR FINESSE' ANALYSIS WINDOW, WHICH DISPLAYS SCOPES WITH REAL-TIME UPDATE.

:: THE TOOLS

The following tutorials demonstrate how several tools perform the primary stages of color correction.

Example 1: Levels

This pane resembles the standard Levels effect, except with two histograms: Input on the left and Output on the right. Input adjustments define white, black, and gamma points. The Output controls work the same but display a histogram reflecting adjustments made in the other tabs, except for Secondary and Limiting. Levels is useful for expanding the tonal range of low-contrast footage. **(SEE FIGURE 31.)**

1. Launch After Effects and open the ColorCorrect project if it's not currently open.

2. Load the 07_ColorFinesse_Levels composition, located in the Tutorials folder.

30 » AFTER COLOR FINESSE LEVELS ADJUSTED.

34 » VECTORSCOPE DISPLAYS A YELLOW-GREEN COLOR CAST.

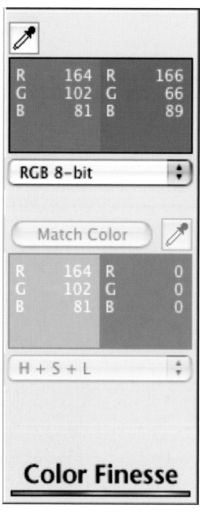

35 » COLOR FINESSE'S COLOR INFO WINDOW

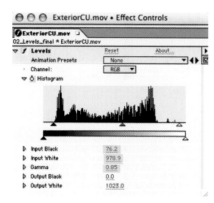

31 » COLOR FINESSE LEVELS PANE. MOST ADJUST-MENTS ARE MADE ON THE INPUT SIDE.

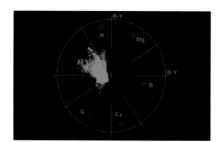

32 » VECTORSCOPE DISPLAYS A YELLOW-GREEN COLOR CAST.

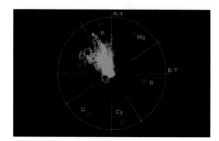

33 » VECTORSCOPE DISPLAY AFTER THE YELLOW-GREEN COLOR CAST IS NEUTRALIZED.

1. In the Timeline window, select the ExteriorCU.mov layer. Let's adjust the tonal range and remove the color cast.

2. Choose Effect>Synthetic Aperture>SA Color Finesse.

3. Click the Setup button in the Effect Controls window to launch the UI.

4. Click the Luma WFM pane in the Analysis window.

5. In the Settings window, click the Levels pane and then click the Master pane.

6. On the Input histogram, drag the black triangle (far left) to the right. Drag the White triangle (far right) to the left. Nudge the Gamma triangle (middle) slightly to the right.

7. Click the Vectorscope pane in the Analysis window. Blacks, whites, and gray should appear in the center of the vectorscope, not toward green and yellow.

8. To neutralize the greenish yellow color cast, click the Green pane in the Levels pane.

9. Drag the black triangle to the right and the gamma to the right.

10. Click the Blue pane and drag the gamma to the left.

11. Click the Red pane. Drag the white triangle to the left and nudge the gamma triangle to the right.

36 » BEFORE COLOR FINESSE CURVES ADJUSTED.

12. To see a final correction, refer to 02_Levels_final composition located in the Final folder.

13. Color-correct the Exterior_still.tif image in the 07_ColorFinesse_Levels composition. Use the 07_ColorFinesse_Levels_final composition as a reference. **(SEE FIGURES 32–35.)**

   [Hint: To trouble shoot a color cast, use the eyedropper to sample the color value for the whites and darks.]

Example 2: Curves

Curves works similarly to the standard Curves effect, only it's easier to control. Any one of the four graphs can use up to 16 control points to narrow the range of values being adjusted. The Match Color feature is also available as a way to establish a base correction for problematic footage. **(SEE FIGURE 38.)**

1. Load the 08_ColorFinesse_Curves composition located in the Tutorials folder.

2. In the Timeline window, select the leisure2.mov layer. This clip is too dark and has a red color cast.

3. Choose Effect>Synthetic Aperture>SA Color Finesse.

37 » AFTER COLOR FINESSE CURVES ADJUSTED.

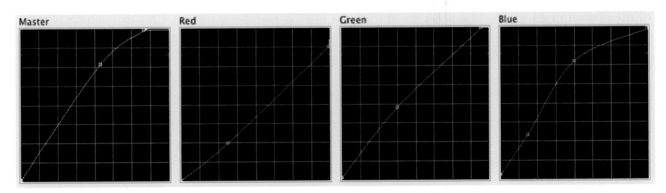

38 » 08_COLORFINESSE_CURVES_FINAL

Histograms	dark_room.tif	TIFF	Project footage
Level Curves	entry.mov	QuickTime Movie	Project footage
Ref Gallery	ExteriorCU.mov	QuickTime Movie	Project footage
	Exterior_still.tif	TIFF	Project footage

39 » COLOR FINESSE'S REF GALLERY IS LOCATED IN THE ANALYSIS WINDOW.

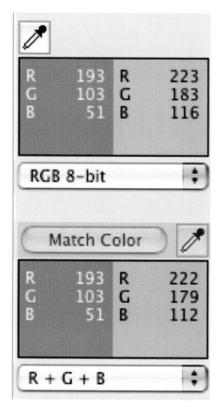

40 » COLOR FINESSE'S COLOR MATCHING CONTROL. THIS CONTROL CANNOT BE USED IN SOME PARAMETER PANES.

4. Click the Setup button in the Effect Controls window, and click the Luma WFM pane in the Analysis window.

5. Click the Curves pane in the Settings window.

6. Adjust the tonal range first. In the Master graph, drag the existing black white point (upper right) to the left. Add a control point by clicking the line, and drag to make a gamma adjustment.

7. Add additional control points to isolate the shadows or highlights.

8. Click the Vectorscope pane in the Analysis window.

   Note: When adjusting the skin tones, the display should move so it's positioned on the I line (the line between yellow and red).

9. To remove the red color cast, adjust the red, green, and blue graphs as shown.

10. (Optional) Use the Match Color feature to establish a base skin tone correction.

Create a reference shot by selecting a shot from the Ref Gallery pane in the Analysis window. Click the Reference tab in the Image window. In the Curves pane, click the eyedropper above the lower color swatches and sample the replacement color. Click the eyedropper above the top color swatches and sample the color to be replaced. Click the Match Color button. Tweak the graphs. (SEE FIGURES 39-41.)

Example 3: HSL

This toolset resembles a traditional color-correction tool palette. It contains two panes: Controls for tonal range adjustments and hue offsets for correcting color casts. The HSL pane works well when neutralizing skin tone color.

1. Load the 09_ColorFinesse_HSL composition located in the Tutorials folder.

2. In the Timeline window, select the Interview_MS.mov layer.

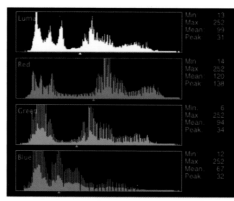
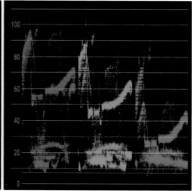

41 » HISTOGRAMS AND RGB WFM.

3. Choose Effect>Synthetic Aperture>SA Color Finesse.

4. Click the Setup button in the Effect Controls window, and click
    the Luma WFM pane in the Analysis window.

5. In the Settings window, click HSL pane, then the Controls pane,
    and finally the Master pane.

6. Drag the RGB Gain slider to the right.

7. Click the Shadows tab. Drag the Gamma slider to the left.

8. Click the Highlights pane. Drag the Brightness slider to the left.

9. Click the Vectorscope pane in the Analysis window.

10. In the Settings window, click the Hue Offsets pane. Adjust the
    shadows, highlights, and then gamma by dragging the central
    black square of each wheel. For better control, hold the Shift key
    to make smaller adjustments. (SEE FIGURE 44.)

    [Note: Color Finesse has several other adjustment tabs with slid-
    ers. See the manual for more information. The Secondary and
    Limiter panes are covered later.]

:: COLOR STABILIZER:

This Pro filter compensates for color variation over time due to
lighting shifts or film flicker. A region is selected from a reference
(pivot) frame. The remaining frames of the image are then adjusted according to the criteria assigned to the pivot frame.

42 » BEFORE COLOR FINESSE HSL ADJUSTMENTS.

43 » AFTER COLOR FINESSE HSL ADJUSTMENTS.

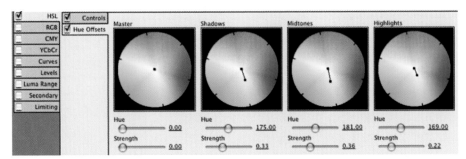

44 » 09_COLORFINESSE_HSL_FINAL

11_BlendModes_final							
0;00;04;05 (29.97 fps)							
		#	Source Name	Mode	T	TrkMat	Parent
👁	▷ □	1	□ Adjustment	Normal ▼			🔗 None ▼
👁	▷ □	2	📄 interview2....	Screen ▼		None ▼	🔗 None ▼
👁	▷ □	3	📄 interview2....	Normal ▼		None ▼	🔗 None ▼
👁	▷ □	4	📄 interview1....	Normal ▼		None ▼	🔗 None ▼

45 » 11_BLENDMODES_FINAL TIMELINE STRUCTURE

:: AUTO FILTERS

After Effects 6.5 includes three additional Photoshop adjustment filters: Auto Color, Auto Contrast, and Auto Levels. These can introduce undesirable results and may need some additional adjustments, which is why they're covered here. The auto filters should be reserved for projects due yesterday. To apply them, choose Effect>Adjust.

Auto Color: Manipulates a clip's contrast and color after analyzing its shadows, midtones, and highlights. Clicking the Snap Neutral Midtones checkbox attempts to neutralize a color cast.

Auto Contrast: Affects a clip's contrast by

Auto Color
Auto Contrast
Auto Levels
Brightness & Contrast
CC Threshold
CC Threshold RGB
Channel Mixer
Color Balance
Color Stabilizer
Curves
Hue/Saturation
Levels
Levels (Individual Controls)
Photo Filter
Posterize
Shadow/Highlight
Threshold

remapping its lightest point to white and its darkest point to black, without removing or generating a color cast.

Auto Levels: Remaps an image's lightest and darkest point for each color channel to white and black. This is similar to Auto Contrast except it may introduce or remove a color cast.

:: BLENDING COLOR CORRECTION

Up to this point, this chapter has focused on the first stage of color correction. Once this primary correction is complete, the tools added to the toolbox can work in conjunction with other After Effects features to make further adjustments or create specific styles. The following tutorial steps through creating a soft film look to match an image shot with a camera using a diffuse filter.

1. Open the 11_BlendModes composition in the Tutorials folder.

2. Perform a primary color correction on interview2, using any of the effects discussed in this chapter. Be sure to adjust tonal range and neutralize the red color cast.

3. Click the interview2 layer in the Timeline and choose Edit>Duplicate. Rename the clips if desired.

4. Select layer 3. Choose Effect>Blur & Sharpen>Fast Blur. Raise the blur amount to about 30.

5. Click the Switches/Modes button at the bottom of the Timeline. Select Screen from the Mode menu on layer 2.

6. Adjust the blur and color filter on layer 3 until the shot matches interview 1. Alternatively, choose Layer>New>Adjustment Layer to provide greater flexibility in tweaking the effect.

7. Refer to 11_BlendModes_final to explore the completed effect. (SEE FIGURE 45.)

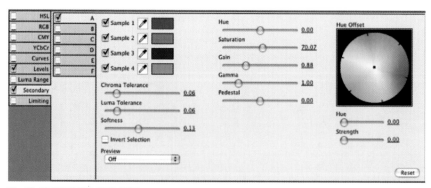

46 » 13_COLORFINESSE_SPOT_FINAL

TIP // Use adjustment layers to separate the shot-to-shot consistency phase from stage 1 and 2.

47 » BEFORE BLEND MODE ADJUSTMENTS.

:: SHOT-TO-SHOT CONSISTENCY

The Blend Modes tutorial is an example of shot-to-shot consistency. In this stage it's important to select one element or clip to serve as a benchmark or reference for correcting surrounding elements. If the reference shot changes, this stage may need to be redone. Any filter covered in this chapter can be used during this stage.

:: SECONDARY CORRECTION

Spot correction involves isolating a specific color of a shot and altering its hue or saturation or both. This technique can be used during stage 4 (create a style) or during an earlier stage when troubleshooting particularly challenging footage. Spot correction can be achieved by combining mattes and color correction filters, or it can be achieved through Synthetic Aperture's Color Finesse, which is explored here.

48 » AFTER BLEND MODE ADJUSTMENTS.

1. Open 13_ColorFinesse_Spot composition in the Tutorials folder.

2. Choose Effect>Synthetic Aperture>SA Color Finesse. Perform a primary color correction on interview1.mov using the techniques highlighted in this chapter. Be sure to adjust tonal range and neutralize the red color cast.

3. In the Settings window, click the Secondary pane.

4. Let's lower the sweater's saturation. Select the eyedropper next to Sample 1 in pane A and sample the woman's red sweater. To see the selection, drag the Hue slider until a color change is visible. Use the remaining three eyedroppers to add to the selection.

5. Select Alpha from the Preview pop-up menu. Adjust the Chroma Tolerance, Luma Tolerance, and Softness sliders until the sweater is essentially the only region selected.

6. When satisfied, Select Off from the Preview pop-up menu, make necessary tweaks, and set Hue to 0.

49 » AFTER SPOT CORRECTION.

50 » BROADCAST COLORS EFFECT. USE IF THE PROJECT IS DUE YESTERDAY.

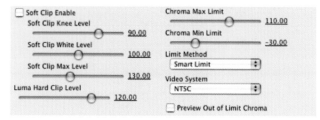

51 » COLOR FINESSE'S LIMITING PANE

7. Adjust the Saturation, Gain, Gamma and Hue sliders until the red in the sweater is subdued.

8. Refer to 13_ColorFinesse_Spot_final to explore the completed effect.

9. For further practice apply the Secondary pane controls to the Exterior_still.tif.

   [Note: The Secondary CC tab pane sliders are organized into three sections. The left side of the effect defines the input color (the color to change), and the middle and right side defines the output color (the color to change to).]

:: FINAL CONFORM AND FINAL WORDS

Once the footage has been corrected and stylized, it's important to make sure it complies with broadcast specifications. These specifications should be kept in mind throughout the compositing process. To ensure that a composition complies, place an auto correct filter on an adjustment layer. Choose Effect>Video>Broadcast Colors. Or you can apply Color Finesse and make adjustments in the Limiting pane.

[Note: The Broadcast Colors effect doesn't support 16-bit color.]

This chapter can serve as a reference and quick guide to color-correction in After Effects. Several excellent books and articles dive deeper into the process. All these resources are great guides, but in the end time spent with the tools will help seamlessly integrate this workflow into your artwork. Building on each experience makes color correction easier.

ABOUT THE AUTHOR

Marianne is a freelance editor who frequently taps into After Effects' color correction tools when constructing motion graphics. She's also a certified instructor who teaches color correction courses. And as a speaker at such conferences as NAB's Post Production World, she's presented several sessions on color correction.

FURTHER READING

Photoshop CS for Nonlinear Editors

Final Cut Pro On the Spot

Photoshop Dream Team Volume One

Photoshop CS2 Killer Tips

Broadcast Graphics On the Spot

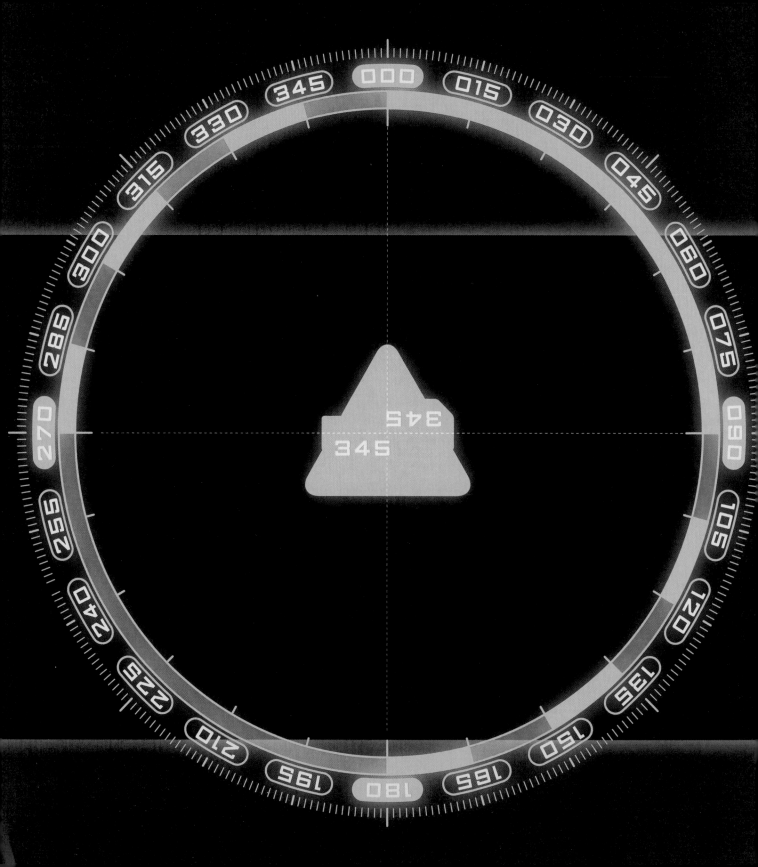

GYRO CONTROL

MARK COLERAN

The core of my work involves the design and creation of computer graphics and heads-up displays for film. Wherever possible, I attempt to break down these screens into components and toolkits, with their own set of controls so they can be quickly and easily adapted for changes, to alternate scenes and other projects. Remember, it's good to recycle!

The following outline is a breakdown of the creation of one of those elements. It involves a few little tricks and some basic techniques that can save you a great deal of time. It also touches on basic expressions that anybody who knows how to copy and paste can understand and use.

WHAT'S ON THE DVD

The DVD contains the project files used within this tutorial. As well as artwork and the beginning and end projects there are saved versions from the various stages. If needed you can open these up for clarification of steps and process.

:: Artwork / Gyro_art.ai

PROJECT FILES ::

:: Stage 1_imported.aep
:: Stage 2_organized.aep
:: Stage 3_shape.aep
:: Stage 4_shape.aep
:: Stage 5_control.aep
:: Stage 6_control.aep
:: Stage 7_control.aep

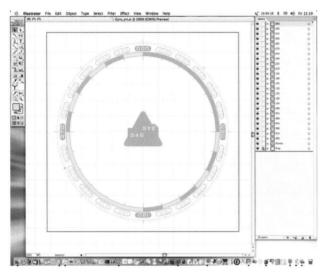

01 »

The Artwork

The artwork for this project has been created in Adobe Illustrator CS. Although we will not go into a discussion on how to create artwork in Illustrator for animation in After Effects, there is one thing that needs to be stated clearly. When creating artwork, think about how it is going to be animated and what you need to create to achieve that end. It is easy to just create artwork, throw it into After Effects and then realize that not all the elements are on their own layers. I know I've done it a thousand times. It is much harder to change this after the event, and sometimes it requires you to restart the After Effects work from the beginning after making major changes to the artwork. Forward planning is always the key.

The other major thing that you can do to make your life far easier is to logically name all the artwork layers in Illustrator. This can pay dividends during work, when it comes to looking at your project and being able to tell rapidly which element is which. It is far easier to read Line work layer 1 and Text Layer 2 over Untitled 1 and Untitled 2.

For this project we are using an element created in Adobe Illustrator consisting of 26 layers. From this we intend to make a 3D gyro-type device. The numbered layers from 000 to 345 are to create a ring around the main ring and the pointer. **(SEE FIGURE 01.)**

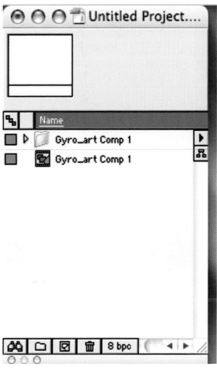

02 »

Tutorial

:: THE PROJECT

First thing for us to do is import the artwork into After Effects.

Start a new project and either double-click in the project bin window or choose File>Import>File.

Select Gyro_art.ai. Before you import it though, be sure to make sure that Import As is set to Composition - Cropped Layers. **(SEE FIGURE 02.)**

Why? We want After Effects to import our artwork exactly as it is laid out in our original artwork. Importing as composition will create a new After Effects project and bring in the same layered structure as the artwork.

Save your file.

:: SAVED PROJECT - STAGE 1 IMPORT

Open the composition Gyro_art Comp 1. You will see the same layer structure from the Illustrator file and all with nice names that tell you what they are.

Now we need to get organized. First we need to flick some switches. Switch all the layers to continuous rasterization.

Then toggle the 3D mode switch so that all the layers will work in 3D space. **(SEE FIGURE 03.)**

03 »

04 »

05 »

06 »

07 »

It will also be easier to to work with this artwork if the project is slightly larger. Press Cmd-K (Ctrl-K) to open the Composition Settings dialog box and type a value of 450x450 for width and height. While you are here you can also double-check that the frame rate and the duration are correct. For this piece we will use a duration of 10 seconds and a frame rate of 24fps.

Why? When you import artwork into After Effects, from either Illustrator or Photoshop as a composition, After Effects creates the new project settings for frame rate and duration based on the last project you created.

This is also a good time to make any changes to the composition name, as it will be difficult later. **(SEE FIGURE 04.)**

:: PROJECT STAGE 2: ORGANIZE

We can now go about setting up our 3D device.

It will be easier to see what you are doing if you change your current artwork view in the main comp window. Change the view from Active Camera to Custom View 2 so that it looks like you are looking down on your artwork. **(SEE FIGURE 05 & 06.)**

For the sake of clarity we will also turn off the visibility of the layer Pointer. **(SEE FIGURE 07.)**

The first thing we are going to tackle are the small blocks that make up the majority of the layers. We want to use these to create a ring around the gyro. It is, however, pretty hard just to move these into a circular position by hand.

When the artwork was created, I knew how large this ring, constructed from the numbered block layers was going to have be in order to go around the outer edge of the ring layer. We can now use this value to rapidly set up this block ring.

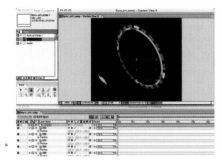

08 »

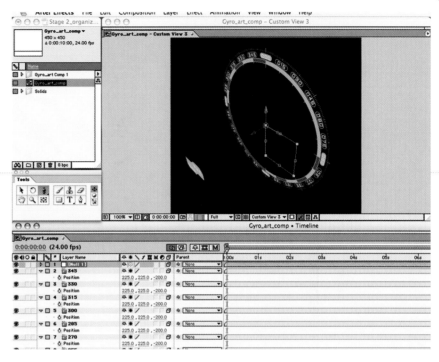

09 »

Select all the block layers (the layers named 000 through to 345) and press P once to see the positions values for all these layers. We can now change the position to the known artwork size value, which in this case is 200. Insert into the Z value −200 and press return. All the layers have now jumped forwards by 200.

Create a new null object from Layer>New>Null Object. Null objects are handy objects that allow you to organize and structure objects in 3D space but that do not show up when you render them. Change to Null to 3D object by switching the 3D toggle in the timeline window. **(SEE FIGURE 08 & 09.)**

Now reselect all the number blocks and parent them to this null. **(SEE FIGURE 10.)**

Select the null layer and press R to reveal the rotation values for the layer. **(SEE FIGURE 11.)**

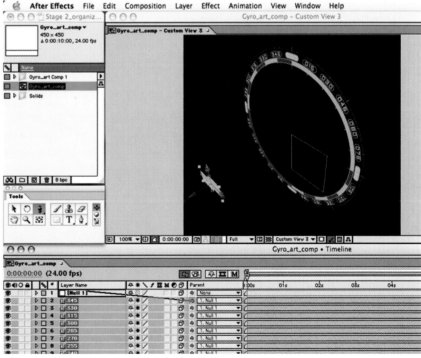

10 »

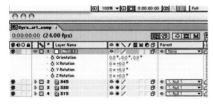

11 »

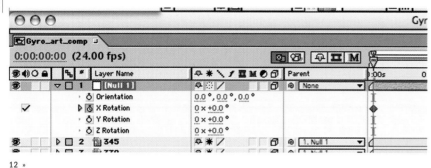

12 »

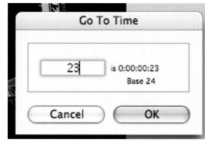

13 »

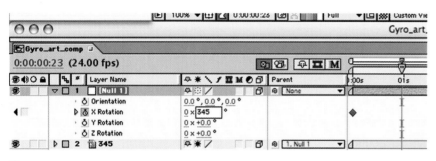

14 »

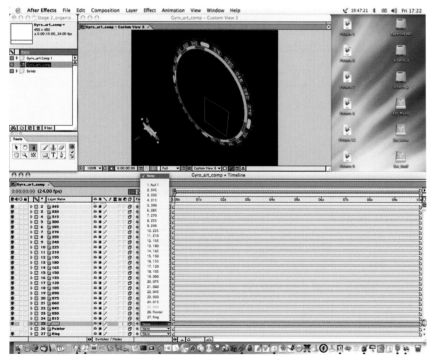

15 »

What we are going to do here is use animation to set up our artwork rather than just use animation for the final output.

Click on the stopwatch to set a keyframe on the X Rotation at 0 frames. Click on the time display on the Timeline to bring up the Go To Time dialog box and type a value of 23. When the Timeline is at this time, click on the angle value for X rotation and set it to –345. **(SEE FIGURE 12-14.)**

[Go back to the beginning of the Timeline and un-parent the first number 000. Move one frame using the Page Down key or your time control panel and then un-parent the next number 015. Repeat for all other blocks. By un-parenting the block we are dumping the blocks where they were at that point in time of parent. It just so happens that the amount of frames used to rotate the null are the same num-

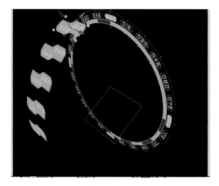

16 »

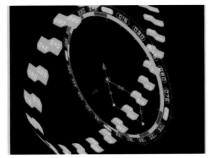

17 »

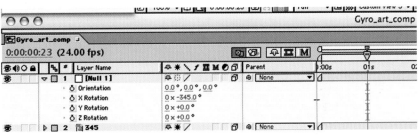

18 »

ber of pieces that we wish to distribute. **(SEE FIGURE 15.)**

It is good to consider the possibilities offered by using animation to set up artwork. **(SEE FIGURE 16.)**

Once you have distributed all block layers, **(SEE FIGURE 17.)** you will want to parent them once again to the null layer. But before you do, set the time at 0 and click on the stopwatch on the null layer's X rotation to remove the keyframes and animation. **(SEE FIGURE 18-20.)**

It can be a good idea just to scrub an angle value for your null layer just to make sure you got all the artwork elements you wanted to parent in place.

Next up we want to set up the two rings for the other two axes. Instead of going through the hassle of creating two rings in the artwork we can just duplicate the single ring we have.

19 »

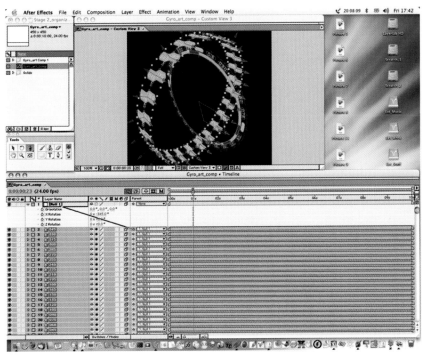

20 »

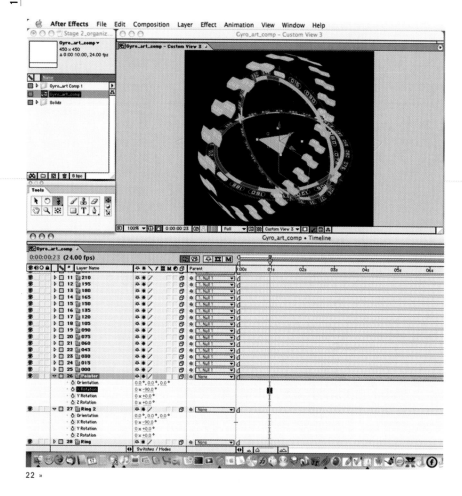

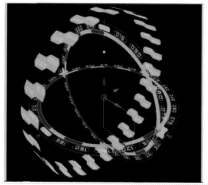

21 »

Select the Ring layer in the Time-line and just press Cmd-D (Ctrl-D) or Edit>Duplicate. This will create a new layer. Press R to see the rotation values of this new layer. Set the X rotation value to −90. We can also turn on the visibility of the Pointer layer and repeat this process. Press R and set the X rotation to −90. (SEE FIGURE 21 & 22.)

:: PROJECT STAGE 3: SHAPE

Right now our image looks complete. but for the sake of easily animating this, we need to make some final organizing touches.

We are just going to create a single null object to link all the other elements to so we can animate it as a single object.

22 »

23 »

24 »

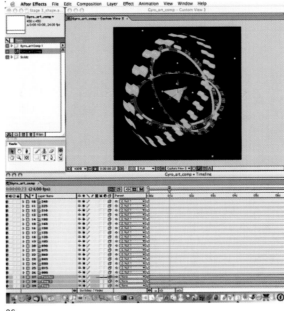

Create a new null from Layer>New>Null Object. Press Cmd-Shift-Y (Ctrl-Shift-Y) to edit the null object's name and rename it Master Null **(SEE FIGURE 23 & 24.)**

Select Null 1 and pickwhip it to the Master Null. Select Pointer, Ring, and Ring 2 and parent them to Master Null. You can now use this null object to control and move the gyro. Select Master Null and press R to reveal its rotation properties. If you want to you can resize the outer block ring so that it sits within the rings by altering the scale of Null 1. **(SEE FIGURE 25 & 26.)**

:: PROJECT STAGE 4: SHAPE

Now, we could just leave it at that. The artwork is set up and ready to rock. But wait, there's more. If we can get After Effects to help set up out artwork for us, why not get After Effects to do the animation for us?

This is where we get into basic expressions. Expressions are not something to

25 »

26 »

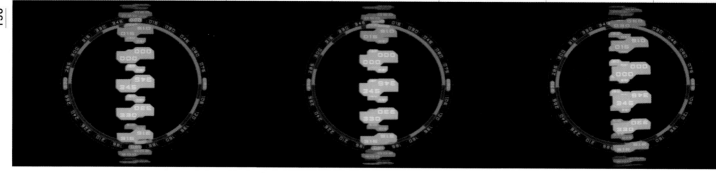

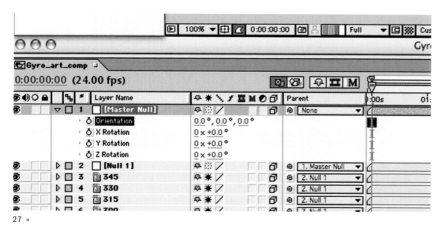

27 »

28 »

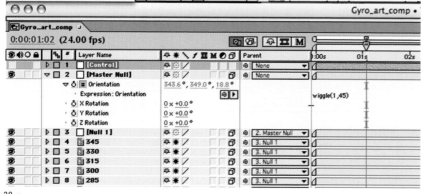

29 »

be scared of. When you go to a foreign country is unnecessary to be able to speak the language fluently, but it can make life so much easier and more rewarding if you have a basic grasp of the local lingo. The same can be said for expressions.

Most people don't want or don't have the ability to think about any type of coding, but here we will use just one simple expression that has over the years saved me countless hours of painful keyframing and will essentially do your animation for you.

WHAT'S NEXT?

Click on Master Null and press R to reveal the Rotation properties. Select the orientation property to highlight it and select Animation>Add Expression. **(SEE FIGURE 27 & 28.)**

The equals sign next to the stopwatch mean that there is an active expression applied to that property. In the bar that has appeared in the Timeline we want to type, replacing the current contents "wiggle [1,45]". Either click away from the type or press Enter to commit the expression.

If you now do a RAM Preview, you will see that the gyro is animated. Work done! But not quite yet.

Let's have a look at the expression. Wiggle is a random-number generator that make a smooth move between the numbers it generates. The values we put into the brackets [1,45] tell the Wiggle how to make the random numbers. In our case it will generate a random number between 45 and −45   once a second. Values of [2,45] would do the math twice a second, and values of [0.5,45] would do the math every two seconds. With a little craft you can get the speed you need that fits perfectly with your desired animation.

The problem with this is that we rarely require an animation just to randomly move. We need some degree of control so it can perhaps start from a very gentle move and speed up. As it stands we cannot keyframe the expression amount, but there is a workaround that introduces you to a concept that I use extensively in my work: the control layer.

This is a layer that I use to animate and control every element and property in a project. Instead of hunting about in all the layers I only go to one place.

Let's start with our own control layer. Create a new layer by pressing Cmd-Y (Ctrl-Y) or choosing Layer>New>Solid. Give the layer a logical name, Control. It doesn't matter how big it is. Turn off the visibility of this solid. **(SEE FIGURE 29.)**

While the layer is still selected, choose Effect>Expression Controls and select Slider Control. This has added what appears to be an effect called Slider Control. Expression controls are ways of generating a value based on the properties you are already familiar with, such as sliders and angles. Although on their own they do nothing, combined with expressions they become extremely powerful. If you press E while the control layer is selected, it will reveal this property. Press Return to rename this layer to wigg_01_time. While this effect is still selected press Cmd-D (Ctrl-D) to duplicate it. Rename this one to wigg_01_amount. **(SEE FIGURE 30.)**

If you look at the layer below Control, the Master Null, we are going to modify the expression here to give us greater control over the animation. Selecting the text of the expression and holding the mouse

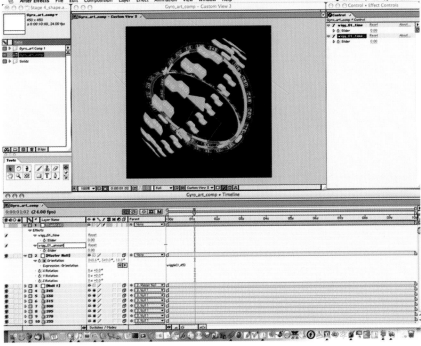

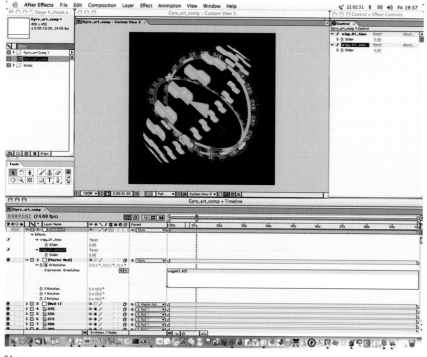

31 »

32 »

over the bottom edge, we can enlarge the expression text area to see the whole expression. Place the cursor on the bottom edge and it will change to a vertical arrow. Pull down the bottom edge so you can see at least three lines of text. (SEE FIGURE 31.)

We will now edit this expression to work with the Slider Controls effect we added to our control layer.

The first thing we need to do is create a variable. A variable is a way of defining a value that is changeable so that we can still use it even though it might be changing. If we have a small equation like 2+2, if it changed to 2+3, we would have to rewrite the equation. If we said, however, that A is the first number and B is the second number then we could just write A+B and would never have to change the equation. It would just be the variables of A and B that would change. Lost you yet?

Placing the cursor at the beginning of the wiggle text, insert two lines above it. Type "T =" and then grab the pickwhip and drag it across to the wigg_01_time Slider value. After Effects will automatically write in the linking code for you. Although it looks complex the expression merely says; in this composition, on this layer, in this effect, using the value of this slider. Using the pickwhip is soooo much easier.

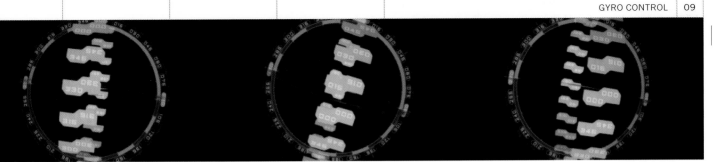

Just remember to add a semicolon after this text to tell After Effects that this is the end of a line.

Repeat this for the next line, typing "A = " then pickwhipping the second effect slider value from wigg_01_amount. Add the semicolon to the end of this line.

Your expression should look like this:

T = thisComp.layer["Control"].effect["wigg_01_time"]["Slider"];

A = thisComp.layer["Control"].effect["wigg_01_amount"]["Slider"];

wiggle[1,45]

All we need to do to this to finish it is change the wiggle values to match the variables we created. Replace the "1" with "T" and the "45" with "A".

wiggle[T,A]

Now if you run a RAM Preview, you will see ... nothing.

That is because the sliders by default have a value of 0. Let's change these sliders so they have some effect. Type in or scrub a value of 2 into wigg_01_time. Type in or scrub a value of approximately 30 into wigg_01_amount.

Now run a RAM Preview and you will see the results. The Gyro now looks like it has come from a very badly flown aircraft!

Why bother to go through all this effort to create and expression and set of controls that appear to do exactly the same as one simple expression, applied to a single parameter of the object? Well, for a start we can now keyframe the animation. Drag your Timeline near the start of the comp but not exactly on the start. Click on the stopwatch to make a keyframe for the "wigg_01_amount". Set this keyframe value to 0. Move your Timeline along slightly and set a value of 30. Set another keyframe slightly further along with another value, let's say 60, and then another at 0 before the end of your composition. As you can now see, we have managed to wrangle the randomness and gained control over it. This can be extremely useful. (SEE FIGURE 32–37.)

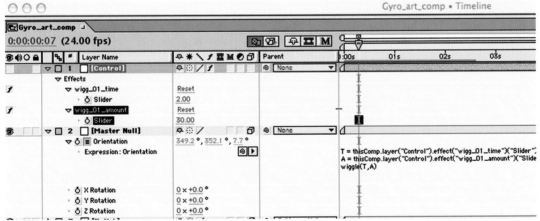

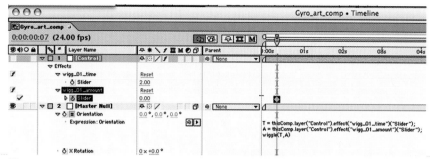

34 »

35 »

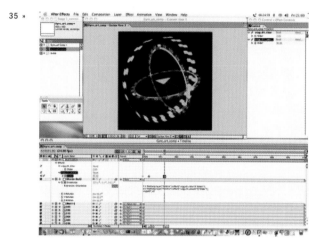

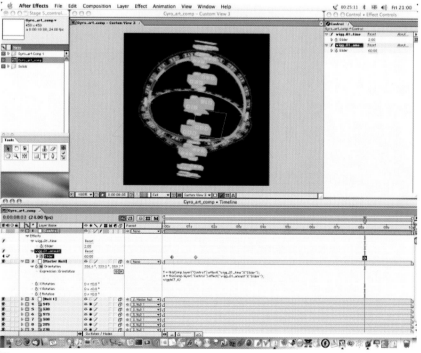

36 »

Let's just reset our keyframe values to something a bit more sedate. Set a value of 0.5 for the wigg_01_time and change the value keyframes for wigg_01_amount to 20.

GOTCHA.... Never set keyframe values for any parameter that involves time. In this case "wigg_01_time". Time is calculated anew each time it changes and would cause the image to randomly jump each and every time it moves to a new frame.

We can now also expand our control and re-use the expression we made to control the object.

Select Null 1 and press R to reveal the Rotation properties if they are not already revealed. Opt-click (Alt-click) on the stop-watch to add an expression. Use the pick-whip to link this value to that of the Master Null, but be careful just to select the first parameter. **(SEE FIGURE 38.)**

What this will do is copy that value into this property, so our Null 1 is rotating on X to the same value as Master Null.

We might, however, want to add a little variety to its motion. All we have to do is go the end of the expression in Null 1 and type *2. This will effectively double the value that we are feeding off. **(SEE FIGURE 39 & 40.)**

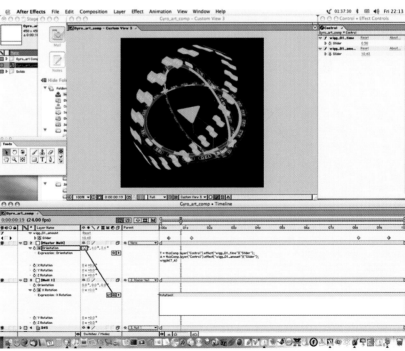

:: PROJECT STAGE 6: CONTROL

If we want to keep this consistent with the way that we have been setting things up here, then instead of putting in an arbitrary value of 2 we should use a variable and give it its own control.

First add another Slider Control. Rename this wigg_extra. Edit the expression to look like this:

E = thisComp.layer["Control"].effect["wigg_extra"]["Slider"];

thisComp.layer["Master Null"].orientation[0]*E

We are adding the variable line, pickwhipping after the equals sign to the wigg_extra parameter and adding the semicolon. On the next line we just change the *2 to *E. You can now set values for this using your control layer. **(SEE FIGURE 38-42.)**

:: PROJECT STAGE 7: CONTROL

We have basically finished putting our Gyro together. It is possible for us to keep

37 »

38 »

39 »

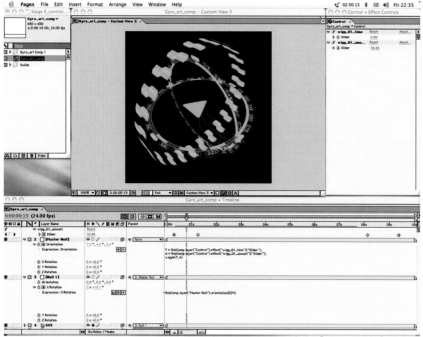

40 »

41 »

adding layers of detail and continually adding to our control layer. It is possible for to even manipulate a large number of our elements at once.

Let add some additional controls to this comp.

Add a new expression control to the layer Control. This time though, add an Angle Control. Rename this block_angle.

NOTE: Naming expression controls is very important. They should always have unique names. This is the reason we used wigg_01_amount earlier. If you wished to create additional wiggle controls then you just count up.

Select Layer 000 and press R to reveal the Rotation properties. (SEE FIGURE 42.)

Opt-click (Alt-click) on the stopwatch to create an expression on the X Rotation parameter and pickwhip this to the block_angle control.

This control will now turn the 000 layer. Not much good on its own! Copy the expression from Layer 000, go to the next layer up, press R and Opt-click (Alt-click) on the stopwatch for the X rotation. Paste the expression into the box. Repeat this for each layer all the way up to 345. (SEE FIGURE 43.)

You now have control of 24 elements from a single point with the bonus that you can also keyframe them from a single point.

There is however one last trick here. It is possible for you to create multiple versions of a composition with only one composition. This can allow you to quickly make huge changes to artwork non-destructively and test different animation options.

Select the layer Control. Press the * key on the numeric keypad to create a marker, double-click on the marker and add a comment, something like version 1. (SEE FIGURE 44.)

Now duplicate the "Control layer". Make sure that it has exactly the same name as the previous control layer. Double-click on

42 »

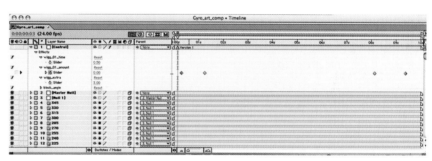

43 »

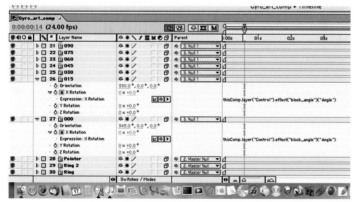

44 »

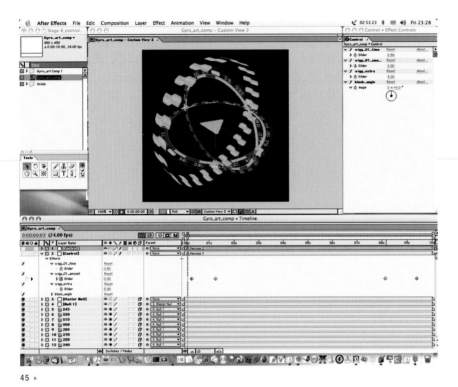

45 »

46 »

the layer marker to change the comment to version 2. **(SEE FIGURE 45.)**

Press Cmd-Shift-T (Ctrl-Shift-T) to open up the effects for this layer. You will see the same controls as for the version 1 layer.

You can now alter the settings and control here as much as you wish.

Here is the payoff, though. Whichever version "Control Layer" is at the top of the Timeline is the version that will get used. **(SEE FIGURE 46.)**

Finishing

As a finishing point the final project has had some additional controls added and a few lights to create a more finished and less flat look. Motion blur switches have been toggled to on.

158

ABOUT THE AUTHOR

Mark Coleran is a motion graphics and visual effects designer for film and television. His clients have been as diverse as the BBC and The Cartoon Network through to the creation of computer interface graphics for feature films such as *The World Is Not Enough*, *The Bourne Identity*, *Blade 2*, and *Aliens versus Predator*. He is also the founder of the online, commercial motion graphics resource Layerlab. For more information and to see a portfolio, go to www.coleran.com.

MAKING A MUSIC VIDEO

KEN LOCSMANDI, FILMWORKS/FX

We'll be attacking this lesson from a do-it-yourself mindset. The video I will be showing is for a band named Key to Arson, for the song "One Last Night." I co-directed the video with David Alexander. The concept behind this video was to shoot a majority of it on greenscreen using a virtual environment. Shooting this way is usually more expensive than shooting it practically. "Practically" means without visual effects, where everything is done in camera. Proficiency in a 3D software package allows virtual environments to be created modestly, and good preparation greatly increases the chances of success. Some key things to consider when making virtual environments are:

• What is your deadline? If you have only a few days or a week you better pull back your ambitions. Good work takes time. Even though the software is good, there is not a magic button that does the work for you. Most directors who use visual effects have a limited understanding of what it takes to create them. The good directors listen to the visual effects team in preproduction and do what is asked of them while shooting.

• Are the rendering times going to kill you? In the "One Last Night" video we created computer-generated (CG) water. Since we had already done water on such projects as Smashmouth's Pacific Coast Party, JAG, and The Pirates of the Caribbean trailer, we knew what was in store for us. We had already learned how to optimize our files for faster render times.

• Limit your moving camera shots. The more moving cameras you have the less assets you can reuse for compositing. Camera moves need to be tracked, and each render is unique to that shot. Later in the lesson you will see how to quickly use the same assets for multiple shots if you have a locked camera. The more you can share assets, the quicker you can get things done and the more time you'll have to be creative.

Preproduction

Almost all projects have problems due to lack of preproduction. When you have a tight budget, preproduction is essential. Having an animatic (moving story board) of the video saves time in production. Instead of using traditional hand-drawn storyboards, a 3D application is used for the animatic. 3D applications like Poser work well. SOFTIMAGE XSI, a high-end 3D application, is $495. It could easily be used for animatics and to make photorealistic digital backgrounds. The advantage of using a 3D application is that real-world data can be incorporated. In this video, the real-world data were the dimensions of the insert stage at Panavision, where the shooting occurred. Measurements were taken, and the stage was built to scale in Alias's Maya. **(SEE FIGURE 01.)**

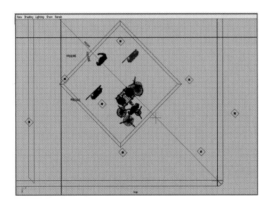

01 »

By having the real-world measurements set up in Maya, we knew where we could shoot, in what direction, and how low or high. In some instances we knew our lens limitations as well. If you know where you are going to shoot, go into your 3D application and make a scene that looks like your shooting area. You don't need to be a great modeler. Just put primitive shapes, but make them the correct size. For example, if you have a person standing on a tree stump that is two feet high, build a cylinder that is two feet high in your 3D application. It's just for reference. We created a simple stand-in model for each band member, and we and color-coded them. We also added the lens that we wanted, along with bits of shot information describing the angle. **(SEE FIGURES 02 AND 03.)**

Angle 1
35 MM

017
01:00:39:29

02 »

We cut the whole thing together with a nonlinear editor with timecode. Now we had a pretty good roadmap. Projects with large budgets typically run through all of the shooting before editing. They may film the entire song dozens and dozens of times. We went through the entire song only twice, once as a wide-angle

performance with a locked camera. The second was a pass with a moving camera. These two setups were backups for editing so the editor would always have something to cut to for artistic preference.

Production

If your budget allows and you know someone who has experience lighting and shooting green, you should see if they can help. If you have to be your own director of photography (DP) then you should know a few things before shooting greenscreen.

03 »

• If possible, shoot in a full frame rate. Film and 24p cameras shoot a full frame. Traditional video cameras shoot fields. These fields are partial information of a full frame. This chapter is not meant to be super technical, so I don't want to get into exact field and frame rate conversions. I will touch the subject briefly once you get into keying the greenscreen.

• Make sure you use the same type of screens on the set. It doesn't mater what type you shoot, whether digital green, chroma green, or bluescreen. Just make sure you are not mixing different types of material.

• Make sure the lighting on the screen is flat. Flat refers to a screen that has consistent lighting across all its areas.

• Keep your subject as far from the screen as possible to limit spill. Spill is greenscreen light reflected onto the subject from the greenscreen. Keying software is very advanced these days, and spill is much easier to correct than in the past.

• Keep objects out of the greenscreen. Remove all objects such as C-stands and ladders. Sometimes it is unavoidable, but many

04 »

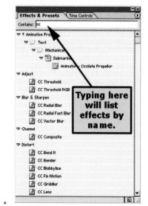

05 »

Effects & Presets — Time Controls

Contains: cc

Typing here will list effects by name.

06 »

Audio | Info

R: 90 X: 691
G: 96 Y: 115
B: 114 +
A: 255

✓ Auto Color Display

Percent (0-100)
Web (00-FF)
HSB
8-bpc (0-255)
10-bpc (0-1023)
16-bpc (0-32768)
Decimal (0.0-1.0)

people get lazy shooting and decide to fix it in postproduction. Don't start that habit.

• The subject should be a different color than your screen. If you are shooting a green car, don't use a greenscreen. It seems obvious, but I have been on many so-called professional sets where things like this happen.

One of the key things that speed up production was having the animatic on set. We took our NLE to the set. Since we had the entire edit with shot information and timecode we could quickly figure out where we were and what we needed to shoot. We hooked the video tape up to a composite input and captured low-resolution images off the film camera. **(SEE FIGURE 04.)**

We would cut in the takes as they were being shot into the appropriate timecode position. You could do this same technique with any editing system on a laptop. Avid Xpress Pro, Adobe Premiere Pro, or Apple Final Cut Pro would work fine. Most laptop computers don't have standard video composite signals, but most have FireWire ports. There are many secondary converters that convert composite video signals to FireWire. We've also used Avid Mojo to bring in footage.

In some cases we would even do rough composites with After Effects. Your greenscreens will never look great coming off a film video tap. If you are using a video camera, you can capture shots and do really good test composites right on set. I've done this while capturing HD footage. The composites almost look like finals.

Postproduction Tutorial

Before you start this lesson you should have a basic understanding of After Effects. Make sure that in the Info window, you have

Auto Display selected. If you have something else selected such as percent, the values given in this tutorial may seem incorrect. One of the main subjects of this lesson is assigning effects. If you leave the Effects window open you can simply start typing the name of the effect in the blank field that has the word contains next to it. As you start to type the effect's name, it will be listed. **(SEE FIGURES 05 AND 06.)**

You are going to do ten tasks. A few of these tasks have subtasks. Here is what will be covered:

1. **Import, interpret, and create a composite**

2. **Clean up and paint out markers**

3. **Pre-compose to make a foreground plate**

4. **Import background elements and compose a composite**

   4a. **Add more TVs**

   4b. **Add volume light**

5. **Bring the foreground and background together.**

   5a. **Pull a key**

   5b. **Get rid of spill**

6. **Isolate and color the tattoo**

7. **Add atmosphere and depth**

8. **Finish final coloring**

9. **Apply all you have done to another shot**

   9a. **Interpret the fields**

   9b. **Make the correct frame length**

   9c. **Add variation**

10. **Output**

SHOT 23 »

Copy the Key to Arson directory from the DVD to your computer.

The first shot I will cover is Shot 23. Shot 23 is the name given to the shot during editing. We had one layer in our NLE that consisted only of shot numbers over the top of our shot image. This gave us a numbering system and a visual guide. Shot 23 was shot from the same angle as Shot 27. All the shots with the same angle can share some assets. These assets can include background images rendered from a 3D application.

Shot 23 and all the shots that have the same angle are locked, which means there are no moving cameras. Later I will show how you can replace footage to finish additional shots quickly. The reason this is possible is because the camera is locked.

:: 1. IMPORT, INTERPRET, AND CREATE A COMPOSITE

Import the footage into After Effects by choosing File>Import>Import File. Choose Local_key_to_arson\RAW\KeytoArson\Key2Arson60_036. Click the first frame of the footage, then check the TGA sequence box at the bottom of the Import window. If you don't check this box, you will get only one frame of the footage. Once the file is imported, we need to convert the footage so that we are working with full frames and not fields. This is known as a 2:3 pulldown. Go to File>Interpret Footage>Main. Assume this frame rate should read 30. Click the Guess 3:2 pull down menu. **(SEE FIGURE 07.)**

After Effects will convert the separate fields into whole frames. All the information for the footage will be displayed in the Project window. The footage is now 24 frames per second (fps). Create a composite using the footage. I like to just drag the footage over the composite icon at the bottom of the Project window (See Figure 22). This will build a composite with the correct length and frame rate. By default After Effects names the composite the

07 »

08 »

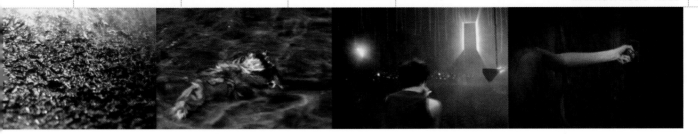

same as the footage. Click the Composite name in the Project window. Press Enter and rename the composite Paint_fix. Save the project as Shot_23.aep. **(SEE FIGURE 08.)**

:: 2. CLEAN UP AND PAINT OUT MARKERS

On set, we put up tracking marks. In this shot they look like little red blobs, but they are actually two pieces of gaffer's tape in the shape of a plus sign or cross. We placed these over the entire greenscreen every three feet before shooting. All the tracking marks have to be removed. **(SEE FIGURE 09.)**

We could draw masks around the marks to remove them, but with this shot we decided that we were just going to paint them out. This is easily done in After Effects. Double-clicking the footage in the Timeline will open it in the Composite window. Select the clone brush. Make sure Mode is set to Normal and Channels are set to RGB. Since this is a locked shot we are going to set the Paint Duration to Constant. **(SEE FIGURES 10 AND 11.)**

The Constant setting will paint all the way through the duration of the shot. Make sure you start painting on the first frame. If you start on frame five then you will see the tracking marks on frames one through four. Pick a brush tip that will cover the entire tracking mark in the image. I used a brush of size 65.

Sample an area of the greenscreen near the marker that you will be painting over. This is done by holding down the Option (Alt) key. Repeat this step for the other unpainted makers. A smaller brush of about 13 could be used for the marker that is under the symbol. Don't paint over the symbol, just the marker. When finished, you will have five clone/paint functions in your Timeline. Expand the attributes on the footage layer in the Timeline by clicking the small arrow next to the name. Add a Remove Grain effect by choosing Effect>Noise & Grain>Remove Grain. The de-

09 »

10 »

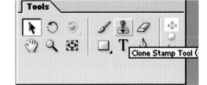

11 »

12 »

fault settings are fine. This will make the shot less noisy, and it will key better. Make sure the viewing mode is changed from Preview to Final Output in the Remove Grain palette. With all the markers gone, we now have clean footage to key. **(SEE FIGURE 12.)**

:: 3. PRECOMPOSE TO MAKE A FOREGROUND PLATE

I'm now going to create a new composite by precompositing my shot Paint_fix. Select the raw painted footage layer in the Timeline. Choose Layer>Precompose and name the new composite Pre_color. Make sure "Move All Attributes into the new composite", is selected. **(SEE FIGURE 13)**

Now there is a composite inside of a composite. The reason this is done is so that we can key on the cleaned composite. Also, this isolates the footage so that later we can easily replace the footage in the composite to complete other shots that are similar.

:: 4. IMPORT BACKGROUND ELEMENTS AND COMPOSE A COMPOSITE.

13 »

Next we'll bring in the CG background plates. They can be found in \Local_key_to_arson\WIP\KeytoArson\Assets\BG_plates.

There are two directories, one called "water" and one called "TV." Import the files from each of the directories. These elements were rendered out of a 3D package and are whole frames at 24fps. There is no reason to worry about pulldown since these files were never video files. The TVs have an alpha channel on them. **(SEE FIGURES 14 AND 15.)**

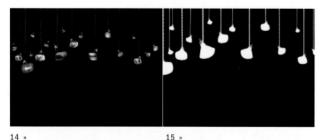

14 »   15 »

After Effects will ask how you want to interpret the alpha channel. Check the Premultiply Matte with Color when importing the TVs. When importing the water check Ignore on the alpha. Interpret both the water and the TV footage as 24fps. **(SEE FIGURE 16.)**

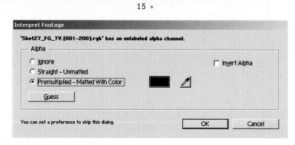

16 »

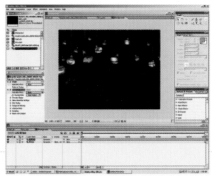

17 »

Make a composite using the water. Name the composite Background. Then drag the TV screen element into the Background composite. Name the TV footage in the Timeline TV_01, and name the water footage Water. You may notice that your composite size is 640X480. We used a square-pixel aspect ratio out of our 3D application. Video has a .9 aspect ratio. Don't worry about this. Everything will size up correctly. (SEE FIGURE 17.)

It may be good to double-check all your composites at this point and make sure they are 24fps.

4a. Add more TVs

Make the Background composite 100 frames long instead of 200. Select the composite and choose Composition>Composition Settings. Change the duration to 100. By making the composite 100 frames long you're able to slide the footage down the Timeline without running out of frames. If your settings are reading in something else instead of frames, go to File>Project Settings and change your preferences to Frame. (SEE FIGURES 18 AND 19.)

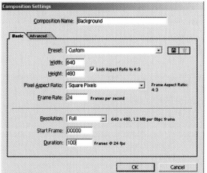

18 »

We want to add more TVs to the scene. With the two elements together the number of TVs seems a bit sparse. Duplicate the TV_01 layer adding more monitors. Since the TV layer is named TV_01, the layer numbers itself automatically to TV_02. Put the new TV layer under the original in the Timeline. (SEE FIGURE 20.) The pixel resolution is 800X600 on the TVs. This was done so that it could be easily scaled and moved if necessary. Scale and reposition the new monitor layers to fill in the scene. I scaled the scene 69% and positioned X as 279 and Y as 232. Your composite should look something like Figure 20. To add a brightness contrast, choose Effects>Brightness Contrast with a brightness setting of 30 on the TV_02 layer. Also, blur them slightly with a fast blur. Choose Effects>Blur & Sharpen>Fast Blur, with a blur-

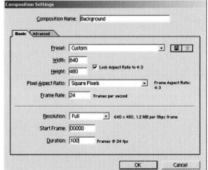

19 »

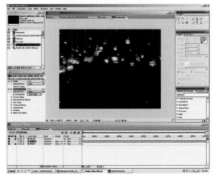

20 »

21 »

Switches / Modes

22 »

Move the
Lightburst
center
here

23 »

24 »

riness of 3. Offset the layer in the Timeline to the left about –70 frames so that the images playing on the TVs in TV_02 look different from those in TV_01. You could go back to the 3D application and fill in more monitors there, but it would require additional 3D rendering times. The beauty of compositing is that you can add things with more layers. So now we have many more monitors, but it looks a little shabby because you can see the edge where the chains stop. Don't worry; the shot is going to have a shallow depth of field, and the background is going to be out of focus. But it still needs more.

4b. Add volume light

We want to give it more volume in the form of light. We're going to build another composite using the background we made. Do this by dragging the background composite onto the Create New Composite icon (SEE FIGURE 21.), in the Project window. This new composite will be named BG_with_light. We need to duplicate the layer BG_with_light, because we're going to add the Cycore Lightburst effect. Choose Effects>Render>CC Lightburst. Applying CC Lightburst to the top layer and changing its blending mode to Screen makes it look as if volumetric light is coming off the TV screens. If you can't find the modes you may have to click the Switches/Modes button (SEE FIGURE 22.) at the bottom of the Timeline. Move the center of the Lightburst to the upper left of the screen. This makes it look like the rays are point down from the TVs. (SEE FIGURE 23.)

On the right side of the composite, the rays look off. Draw a square mask over the left side of the screen so that only the monitors on the left are visible. The light is now shining only from the monitors on the left. (SEE FIGURE 24.)

Duplicate the layer containing the newly drawn mask. Make sure you duplicate the layer and not just the effects. Change the Mask

attribute of the new layer from Add to Subtract. Now the rays on the screen's left side are back, but they are still in the wrong direction. Move this layer's Lightburst center to the upper right. Now the volume light looks as if it is shining correctly. **(SEE FIGURE 25.)**

The light doesn't have to be perfect because the background is going to be blurry. Now there is a base background that has extra monitors and volume light.

:: 5. BRING THE FOREGROUND AND BACKGROUND TOGETHER

We'll now bring our BG_with_light composite into our main composite named Pre_color. With the two layers together we can start keying and combining the elements. Rename the top layer FG. Rename the bottom layer BG. There will be other foreground elements added later. **(SEE FIGURE 26.)**

5a. Pull a key.

Add a key light to the FG layer. Choose Effect>Keying>Keylight. Sample some of the greenscreen using the Eyedropper tool **(SEE FIGURE 27.)** in Keylight palette. A good area to sample is next to the singer's head. Hair is often difficult to make look good, so sampling a green in the general area is an adequate place to start. Keylight does an excellent job very quickly. **(SEE FIGURE 28.)**

In Keylight, set the View to Screen Matte. **(SEE FIGURE 29.)** This shows how well the key worked. Changing the Screen Matte clip

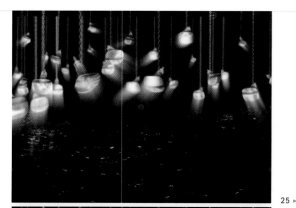

25 »

26 »

27 »

28 »

▸ View	Final Result ▼

29 »

30 »

31 »

32 »

black to 12 and clip white to 71 will help fix some of the bad areas of the matte. Most beginners try to make the matte completely white and black. This will cause loss of detail in the image. The matte can be slightly dirty, containing gray values. Once you start adding all the additional elements of the composite, you'll find that it is not necessary to make the matte really tight (all black and white). (SEE FIGURES 30 AND 31.)

Once you have a fairly good matte, turn the View back to Final Result. The image will start to look a bit grainy. Turn down the screen balance setting in Keylight to about 33. It's less grainy, but some of the green spill made it back into the image. (SEE FIGURE 32.)

5b. Get rid of spill

The foreground image still has bounced light from the green-screen on it. This is known as spill. An additional color balance effect will remove more green from the shadows and midtones. Choose Effects>Adjust>Color Balance. The adjustment is very minor, only –3.0 to the green shadows and green midtones. (SEE FIGURE 33.)

:: 6. ISOLATE AND COLOR THE TATTOO

The key has made the color of the tattoo look bland. Most of the green is now gone. We'll create another layer by duplicating the Paint_fix layer to compensate for the color shift. Remember, the Paint_fix layer was renamed FG in the Timeline.

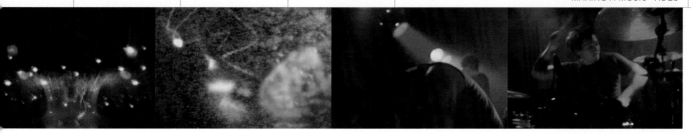

Name the new layer "Tattoo" and delete all its effects. Just select the effects in the layer and press Delete on the keyboard. Drawing a rough mask around the tattoo with a feather of about 16 pixels will be sufficient to color it appropriately. A large feather radius allows the mask to be less accurate. Roughly animate the mask so that it follows the tattoo. Click the animation stopwatch on the mask shape (See Figure 32). You don't need to animate every frame of the mask. Start with the first frame, then move to the last, then the middle. Add keyframes in between the ones that seem off. **(SEE FIGURE 34.)**

It doesn't have to be exact because you have a large feather. Add a hue saturation. Choose Effect>Adjust>Hue/Saturation, with an increased master saturation value of about 30. Next, crush the image a bit with a level effect. Choose Effects>Adjust>Levels. The input black level should be around 20, and the input white level should be about 240. Now it looks like fresh ink! **(SEE FIGURES 35 AND 36.)**

« 34

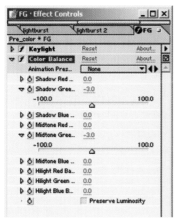

« 33

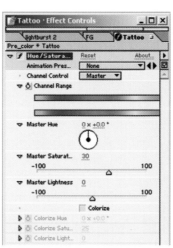

« 35

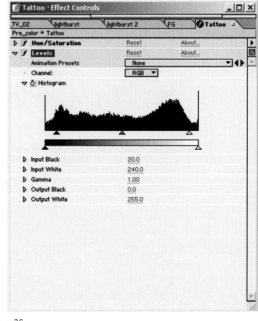

« 36

37 »

38 »

39 »

:: 7. ADD ATMOSPHERE AND DEPTH

We need to add some atmosphere and depth cueing. A smoke element shot on a black background will be used to do this. You can shoot your own elements by having smoke in front of duvetyne, a black non-reflective fabric. You can get stock footage as I have done many times through Artbeats.

Import the smoke from \Local_key_to_arson\WIP\KeytoArson\Assets\Smoke. **(SEE FIGURE 37.)**

Make sure the frame rate is 24fps. If you have ever looked at a mountain range, you may have noticed that the mountains that are further away have more of a grayish tint to them than the ones closer. Traditional painters studied such phenomena and used them in their work. The more you begin to composite the more you need to learn these traditional art skills. We will add a layer of smoke just above the BG layer. Changing the blending mode to Screen will add only the lighter values to the composite. The blackest parts of the smoke layer will become transparent. **(SEE FIGURE 38.)**

An opacity value of 50 on the layer will blend it in, making the background not so dark. This gives it the feeling that it has atmosphere and depth. The drummer still seems a little dark. **(SEE FIGURE 39.)**

Duplicate the smoke layer and make it the top layer. Since we have the blending mode and the transparency levels already set, we don't need to make any adjustments. Put a fast blur with a blurriness value of 6 on the BG layer. This makes the background depth of field balance out with the depth of the drummer. The new layer blends in and adds more of the needed depth. This composite is almost complete.

8. FINISH FINAL COLORING.

We're going to add more of a cool (temperature) look to it. Make an entirely new composite out of the Pre_color composite. Drag the Pre_color comp onto the Make New Composition icon **(SEE FIGURE 40)**. Name the new composite FIN.

40 »

After Effects has something called an Adjustment Layer. This is a non-destructive layer that can hold effects. All the effects applied to the Adjustment Layer will be applied to all the layers under it within the Timeline. Create an adjustment layer. Choose Layer>New>Adjustment Layer. Put a CC Toner on the Adjustment Layer. Choose Effects>Image Control>CC Toner. Manipulate the midtones in the Toner menu from gray to medium blue, and make blend with original 70. Now the color temperature of the light in the composite looks cooler. **(SEE FIGURE 41.)**

41 »

The people now look like they are frozen. The surrounding color is desirable, but the skin needs to be warmer. With the adjustment layer selected, draw some quick junk masks around the people. **(SEE FIGURE 42.)**. Set the Mask Properties to Subtract so that the Adjustment Layer affects the background and not the people. It is not necessary to animate the masks. Adjust the mask feather to 30. Now the people don't look like they are frozen, and the shot is finally finished. **(SEE FIGURE 43.)**

42 »

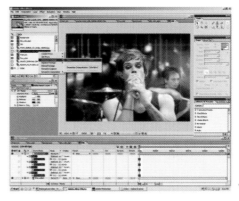

« 43

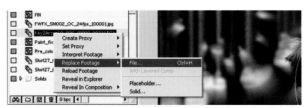

« 44

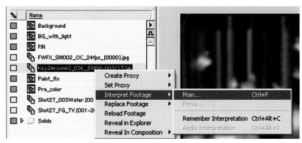

« 45

« 46

:: 9. APPLY ALL YOU HAVE DONE TO ANOTHER SHOT.

We can now quickly finish a few more shots, by just replacing footage and changing the time duration. In the Project window, Ctrl-click (right–click) the RAW greenscreen footage of Shot 23, named KeytoArson60_36 and replace it with the Shot 27 RAW footage, which is named KeytoArson61_37. **(SEE FIGURE 44.)**

9a. Interpret the fields.

Interpret the footage by guessing the 3:2 pulldown for this new Shot 27 footage. The pulldown should be different between the two pieces of footage. **(SEE FIGURE 45.)**

9b. Make the correct frame length.

Shot 23 is 27 frames long. Shot 27 is 44 frames long. The composite frame lengths have to be adjusted in order to make them equal to the shot lengths of the new composites. Right away, re-name this project Shot 27. This will make sure that you don't loose Shot 23. It will also help clear up any confusion. Now we will correct all the lengths of the composites starting with the Paint_fix composite.

Choose Composition>Composition Settings and make the Duration 44 frames. **(SEE FIGURE 46.)**

The strokes in this composite will also have to be stretched to the correct frame length. **(SEE FIGURE 47.)**

This can be done by grabbing the end of the Clone Paint Timeline bar and pulling it to the end of the frame length, which is now 44. Adjust all the other composites so that the footage is extended all the way to the end of the 44 frames. Leave the background composites' frame lengths alone. **(SEE FIGURE 48.)**

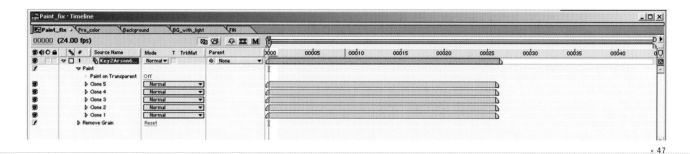

« 47

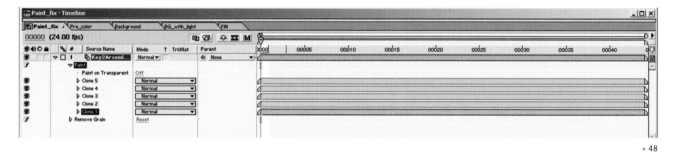

« 48

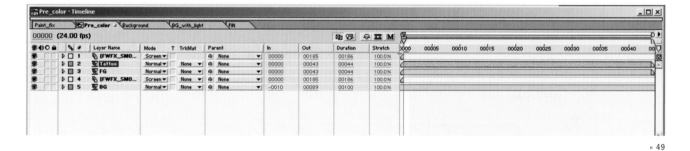

« 49

9c. Add variation.

The background is longer than 44 frames. Having the length of the composite longer allows variation to the animation on the consecutive shots. In the Pre_color composite we'll move the BG layer in the Timeline to the left a few frames; 10 or so should be fine. This offsets the background making it different than Shot 23. (SEE FIGURE 49.)

You may find that some things such as masks need to be corrected. The tattoo layer in Pre_color needs to have its masks adjusted to follow the new footage. **(SEE FIGURE 50.)**

By replacing the footage and adjusting frame lengths, we have another complete shot in just a few minutes. This same procedure can be applied to all the shots that have a similar angle.

:: 10. OUTPUT THE FINAL PRODUCT.

The fields need to be put back into the render in the same order as they were imported. Selecting the raw footage in the project displays all attributes of the footage, including the 3:2 removal information. In order to render the FIN composite you have to add it to the render queue. Choose Composition>Add to Render Queue. With the render queue open, click Best settings to open the render settings. Make sure the quality is set to best and the resolution is set to full. Under time sampling, make sure your 3:2 settings are the same as those in your raw greenscreen footage. In this case the field rendering should be set to Lower Field First, and the 3:2 pulldown should be set to SSWWW. **(SEE FIGURE 51.)**

Click OK. Then choose the output module by clicking on the word Lossless. Select the parameters you need to get the footage back into your NLE. I've set it up to render a TGA sequence. Pick a render directory by selecting Output to Name. Name your files Shot27_[#####].tga. Each # symbol represents the number padding of the frame rendered. Frame one will be, shot27_00001.tga. Frame 44 will be shot27_00044.tga and so on. The shot is finished. **(SEE FIGURE 52.)**

50 »

51 »

Conclusion

Digital compositing is one the most amazing visual effects tools to date. Desktop tools are affordable, accessible, and fairly intuitive. The possibilities are endless. But new tools and faster computers don't make up for an artistic eye. Study traditional art skills. These can be applied to any artistic discipline and are timeless. Don't get frustrated. The challenges of visual effects work enhance the rewards. Most of all, keep having fun. If it's not fun, it's not worth doing.

52 »

⚙ SHOT MANAGEMENT

When working on large projects, it's easy to lose track of your shots. A typical video may have 50 to 100 visual effects shots. Most individuals can't afford to have someone program an asset-management system. Here are a few tips on organizing so you don't get overwhelmed.

// USE AN NLE AS A SHOT ORGANIZER.

Any NLE will work as long as it has the option of superimposing text over clips in a layer. We use an NLE called the Leitch Velocity.

In Velocity, the shots clips are on one layer. Another layer is created with shot numbers that we assign. If the numbers are made large they are fairly easy to see.

(SEE FIGURE 53.)

// COPY YOUR SHOTS TO A CENTRAL LOCATION.

Our server is set up with the following directory structure.

:: R (RAW) drives contain the raw unfettered source footage. This would include the greenscreen clips as they were shot and background plates. Since the background footage was CG we wouldn't have background plates.

:: The W (WIP) drive is where all the data and asset work is stored. WIP is an abbreviation for "work in progress." This directory is backed up nightly.

:: The final drive in our system is the T drive. Temp is short for "temporary." Anything at any time can be deleted from this drive. We have a directory within our temp directory called Deliver. Final composites are rendered to Deliver before they are imported into the NLE.

// MAKE DIRECTORY STRUCTURES THAT KEEP YOU ORGANIZED.

You should formulate a directory structure that works for you. As deadlines approach things begin to get sloppy. If you just randomly start putting your files everywhere, eventually you will lose track and mess something up. My biggest pet peeve is saving files to the desktop. Saving to the desktop usually shows that there is no understanding of file structure at all. Get into a routine of saving your work in the same place and rendering to specific directories. Make a generic directory structure and call it "Template." In that directory make subdirectories that correspond with the shot you are doing and the applications you use. A good way to organize is to duplicate the Template directory and rename it using the shot number from the NLE. Our template contains subdirectories named Maya, Max, After Effects, Zbrush, and Photoshop.

ABOUT THE AUTHOR

ABOUT THE AUTHOR

Ken Locsmandi has worked on several projects including The Matrix, The Cell, and Terminal, as well as many other commercial, television, DVD, and film projects. Ken is co-founder and CFO of Filmworks/FX a full-service post-production facility. The company has film-processing, telecine, editing, and visual effects.

As an animator for the film *Rusty: A Dog's Tale*, for Calico Creations Ken developed techniques for live-action animal scenes that the studio used in its animation pipeline. From 1998 to 2000 Ken's own company Filmworks/FX was contracted on such projects as The Matrix, The Cell, Backstreet Boys, and Janet Jackson music videos, as well as many other commercial, television, DVD, and film projects.

Ken has supervised such projects as Smashmouth's Pacific Coast Party, Lil BowWow's "Basketball," "Slum Village," and "Tainted." Ken won the Omni Award for best visual effects on television for the 2001 season finale of JAG. Ken also won the Slamdunk 2003 film writing competition for his short film script *The Piñata*.

⚙ ON SET, AND ON A TIGHT BUDGET

54 & 55 »

The total budget of this video was $10,000 dollars. It was shot on 35mm film, mostly on a greenscreen stage using Panavision cameras and a techno crane. I happen to own a laboratory and telecine, so shooting on film wasn't an issue. My producers have also been in the film business for years, so they were able to pull in favors on equipment and film stock. (SEE FIGURES 54 AND 55)

You don't need to shoot on film. Don't get discouraged because you don't have all these gadgets. You don't need them. You just need to be creative with what you do have. You can do something very similar using inexpensive tools. A 24p video camera and tripod with a movable head would work great. Even handheld is fine, but tracking a background in is much more difficult. You will still need tracking marks if you're going to move the camera on a tripod or by hand. The following are a list of fairly inexpensive tools.

- :: 24p camera or miniDV camera
- :: Tripod
- :: Red gaffers tape
- :: Greenscreen (paint)
- :: Lighting kit
- :: Good strong back
- :: Optional jib arm
- :: 3D application
  (Alias Maya, Avid SOFTIMAGE XSI, Autodesk 3ds max)
- :: Compositing package (After Effects)
- :: Non-linear editor (Adobe Premiere Pro, Avid Xpress Pro DV, Apple Final Cut Pro)
- :: A crew that will work for pizza

Financial Presentations with Flair
POSTWORKS
Net Sales (in millions)
Post-production
Multimedia
Duplication
300
26%
53%
3%
02
03
04
Rent 26%
Taxes 8%
Equipment
& Software 6%
$

FINANCIALS WITH FLAIR

MICHELE YAMAZAKI

Ever had to wade through stacks of facts and make them look interesting? Although practical, presentation charts can be lifeless and ho-hum. It doesn't have to be that way.

I'm working with graphs that were created in Microsoft Excel by a right-brained person. The client is my company, Postworks, and we're a fresh and dynamic group of left-brainers. The graphs needed to match the personality of our company, so therein lies the challenge.

Only a few years ago, Postworks was a pioneer in DVD. We were the second company in Michigan to author DVDs. We made a DVD for a large company during the time that company went public. The CEO presented the financial graphics to the moneymen, who were used to Microsoft PowerPoint presentations, and they were blown away by this new technology.

This project is the same type of thing: a short opening followed by three financial graphs on DVD that are used as speaker support.

You'll put four to five hours into this project. If you're new to After Effects, I'll cover masking and drawing paths, effects and animation presets, the Advanced Text Engine/ Type tool and some basics of Adobe Illustrator. Before you begin, view the movies on the DVD and get familiar with the project, then skim the chapter before jumping in.

WHAT'S ON THE DVD
:: Microsoft Excel document with exported PDFs
:: Project files organized by folder
:: Rendered final movie
:: Animation Presets

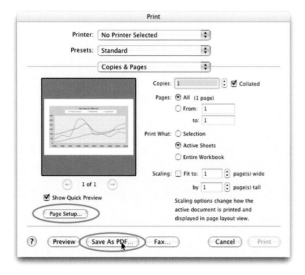

01 » CREATING A PDF ON THE MAC IS EASY USING THE PRINT DIALOG BOX.

Getting Data from Microsoft Excel

First, print the charts. These will be good reference, and you won't have to refer back to the Excel document all the time. Write extra information on the printouts, such as labels that do not show up on the printouts.

Extracting charts from Excel to use in another program is not exactly a simple or elegant matter. Microsoft Office software doesn't always play nice with Adobe software—so, for example, Cut and Paste sometimes fails.

Save the Excel Documents as PDFs on a Mac

I am saving the files as PDFs for reference in After Effects. These PDFs retain vector information, so they could be used in Illustrator. That little tidbit could come in handy in a future project, so file it in your brain. (SEE FIGURE 01.)

1. Open charts.xls in Excel. Choose File>Print. Click Page Setup and set it to Landscape. If your document is too large for the page, like mine is, change the paper size from US Letter to US Legal, then click "OK."

2. Back in the Print dialog box, click the Save as PDF button and name it linegraph.pdf. In newer versions of Excel, you must click OK, then File>Print>Save as PDF. Make sure you uncheck "Hide extension" in the lower-left corner or type ".pdf".

3. If your version of Excel has a checkbox for printing all pages of the workbook, be aware that After Effects can import only the first page of PDF files, so you'll need to repeat this process with each Excel workbook. Click the tabs at the bottom to toggle between them. Save them as piechart.pdf and bargraph.pdf. This is a Mac-only option, but there is a workaround in Windows (see sidebar).

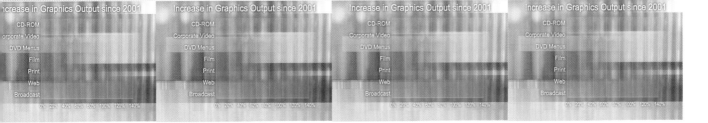

Save the Excel Documents as PDFs in Windows

Print your Office document to PDF using the Adobe Acrobat Distiller print driver.

In Microsoft Excel:

1. **Choose File>Print.**

2. **In the Printer Name pop-up menu at the top of the Print window, choose Acrobat PDF Writer.**

3. **You'll be prompted to save your document. Give it a file name and choose a location to save it.**

4. **Save your document as a PDF.**

   See the Adobe Support Knowledgebase document #322594 for more information (http://www.adobe.com/suppor/tech-docs/322594.html).

Setting Up Your Project in After Effects

I hope you don't get the idea that I'm really anal-retentive. I'm actually one of the messiest people you'll ever meet. My virtual world, however, is always neat and tidy. **(SEE FIGURE 2.)**

1. **Launch After Effects and open Charts.aep, included on the DVD.**

2. **Import your three PDF files by using the shortcut Cmd+I (Ctrl+I). The Import dialog box will open. Import the files as footage. These will be used as reference only.**

3. **Set up the same folder system in your Project window. I created a folder called "elements" and put the PDF files in it. To create a folder quickly, click the folder icon at the bottom of the Project window. A folder will appear called "Untitled 1." Rename that folder by selecting it and pressing the Return key. You can then edit the name. Drag your PDF files into it.**

4. **Start some good habits early and save your project. I saved mine as "charts.aep" in the main financials folder.**

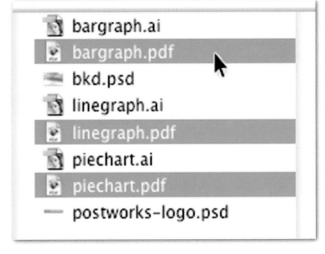

02 » IMPORT MULTIPLE FILES AT ONE TIME BY CMD+CLICKING (CTRL+CLICKING) THE FILES THAT YOU WANT TO IMPORT.

⚙ TITLE SAFE

The title-safe area is the area of the screen where your type will not be cut off on the edges of television screens. Twenty percent of the screen is outside the title-safe area, and 10 percent is outside the action-safe area. One awesome feature of After Effects is that it automatically calculates the proper safe areas, whether you're working in PAL, HD or any screen ratio. This is not as much as an issue with newer flat-panel televisions. If your project will be projected or shown on a computer monitor, you do not need to worry about the title-safe area. So, find out how the video will be shown before you start a project. You could have 20% more real estate to utilize.

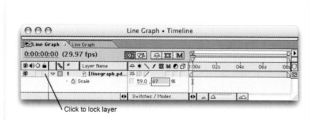

Click to lock layer

03 » UNCHECK THE LINK NEXT TO THE SCALE PERCENTAGES SO THAT YOU CAN CHANGE THE X AND Y VALUES INDIVIDUALLY.

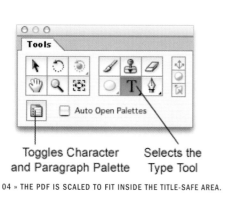

Toggles Character and Paragraph Palette

Selects the Type Tool

04 » THE PDF IS SCALED TO FIT INSIDE THE TITLE-SAFE AREA.

Put in the PDF Guides

First on our list is the line graph. We're going to redraw the graph instead of building it in Illustrator. You'll be just as accurate, and it will be much less of a headache.

1. Create a new comp by using the shortcut Cmd+N (Alt+N). Use the following settings:

   :: Name: Line Graph
   :: Size: Preset NTSC DV, 720x480 (We're setting this up for an NTSC DVD).
   :: Frame rate: 29.97
   :: Duration: 10 seconds (00:00:10:00)
   :: Background color: anything easy on the eyes (mine is light blue)
   :: If you're in the PAL world, check your documentation of your DVD authoring program to see what you'll need.

2. Drag linegraph.pdf into the comp. I scaled it to X=59% AND Y=87%. The proportions are different, but that is okay with the client. Make sure that linegraph.pdf is completely within the title-safe area. Click the checkbox below the lock icon in the A/V settings. This will ensure that you don't accidentally move the PDF guide.

3. Go to the first frame in the Timeline by pressing the Home key. If you're on a laptop and do not have a Home key, click the Current Time indicator on the upper left of the Timeline and go to 0. (SEE FIGURES 3 & 4.)

Add the Background

Normally, I would animate a background, but for the sake of space, I'm going to use a still in this tutorial.

1. Open bkd.psd in the Elements folder.

2. Drag bkd.psd to the bottom of the stack of layers in your Line Graph comp. Make sure it fills the duration.

3. Turn off the visibility of bkd.psd.

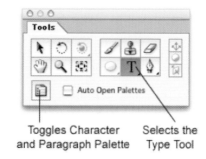

Toggles Character   Selects the
and Paragraph Palette   Type Tool

05 » WHEN THE AUTO OPEN PALETTES BOX IS CHECKED, THE CHARACTER PALETTE WILL OPEN IF THE TYPE TOOL IS CLICKED.

Add the Chart Title

1. Click the Type tool and click in the Project window in the upper center, within the title-safe area. Type "Net Sales (in Millions)." Use the Character palette to adjust the size, tracking, and font and center it using the Paragraph palette.

2. Since this will be shown on a TV screen, it's important to make the type large enough. I set it to 30pt Arial, with the tracking set to -30. Make the text white and position it at the top center of the screen.

3. To speed up this project, we'll use the incredible text presets included in After Effects 6.5. (If you have version 6.0, check out the sidebar "Animating Text in After Effects 6.0" for animation instructions.)

4. Open the Effects and Presets palette Cmd+5 (Ctrl+5). Twirl down Animation Presets>Text>Animate In. Choose Characters Shuffle In. The text disappears at the first frame and animates on (so if you're concerned that your text is gone, it's just off-screen.)

5. We're not going to tweak this effect in the tutorial, but if you'd like to change the speed, move the keyframes farther apart or change the position. (SEE FIGURES 5, 6 & 7.)

6. Apply a drop shadow to the text (Effect>Perspective>Drop Shadow). Change the following settings: Opacity: 100%, Distance: 0, Softness: 15.0. We're going to use these Drop Shadow settings for each text layer that we will make, so to speed things up, we'll save it as an Animation Preset.

7. Double-click the Drop Shadow effect in the Timeline to open the Effects Control window.

8. Pull down the Animation Presets menu and choose Save Animation Preset. The "Save Preset as" window will pop up. Save as "Charts Drop Shadow.ffx". Navigate to your Applications (Programs) folder. Find the After Effects application folder, then the Presets folder. Create a folder called "Charts" and save your preset there.

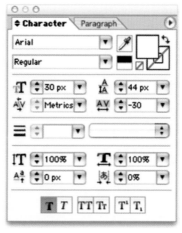

06 » THE CHARACTER PALETTE IS LIKE THE ONE IN PHOTOSHOP. YOU CANNOT SET KEYFRAMES FROM THE CHARACTER PALETTE SETTINGS, SO USE IT TO INITIALLY SET UP TEXT.

07 » STEP 6: AFTER EFFECTS 6.5 BROUGHT SOME USEFUL TEXT ANIMATION PRESETS TO THE PARTY. THEY'RE ADDICTIVE!

SAVING AND APPLYING ANIMATION PRESETS (FAVORITES) IN AFTER EFFECTS 6.0

1. Open the Effects Control Window by double-clicking Drop Shadow in your Timeline.

2. Choose Save Selection as Favorite in the Effect Favorites drop-down menu.

3. Save it in the Favorites folder in your application folder. You can save it in a subfolder called Charts, specifically for this project.

To apply a favorite in After Effects 6.0, choose Effect>Apply Favorite. If it's a recent Favorite, choose Effect>Recent Favorite then choose from the submenu.

ANIMATION PRESETS WERE KNOWN AS EFFECT FAVORITES IN AFTER EFFECTS 6.0.

9. In After Effects 6.5, to apply a preset, drag it from the Effects and Presets window onto your layer. Alternately, go to Animation>Recent Animation Presets and find Charts Drop Shadow.

10. If you haven't saved lately, please do it now.

Speedy Set-Up of the Pie Chart and Bar Graph

I am a big fan of getting things done quickly. The quickest way to get the other two charts going is to duplicate the Line Graph comp.

1. Select the Line Graph comp in the Project window and press Cmd+D (Ctrl+D). A new comp will appear in your Project window called Line Graph 2. Duplicate it again and you'll get a comp called Line Graph 3.

2. Select Line Graph 2 and press Return. This makes the comp name editable. Rename it Bar Graph. Rename Line Graph 3 Pie Chart.

3. Double-click the Pie Chart comp to open the Timeline. Find the file called piechart.pdf in the Project window. Unlock it by unchecking the box below the lock icon.

4. You can easily replace a selected layer's source footage in the Composition window with selected footage.

   :: Select the layer you want to replace in the Timeline. In this case, it's linegraph.pdf. Use the following shortcut:
   :: For Mac, use Command+Option+/
   :: For Windows, use Ctrl+Alt+/
   :: Lock the layer.
   :: Turn on the visibility of the PDF.

5. As you replace the PDF file with the piechart.pdf file, you may notice that your pie chart is not round. Press the S key to bring up Scale and set the scale to 79% for both the X and Y axis. (SEE FIGURE 8.)

6. The background and PDF guide are ready to go; we just need to fix the title. Go to 3:00 in the Timeline, or anywhere in the Time-

line that you can see the whole title in its final position. Press Cmd+T (Ctrl+T) to select the Horizontal Type tool. Drag it across the existing title to select it and type "2004 Expenditures" over top of the Net Sales text. Because this text is shorter than the Net Sales text we're replacing, it will animate slower. Press the U key to bring up Offset, and drag the second keyframe to 1:20.

7. Repeat Step 7 for the Bar Graph and save your project.

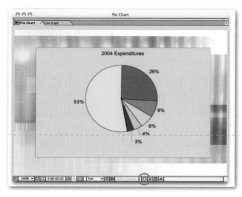

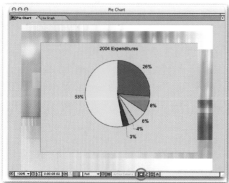

08 » IS YOUR PIE CHART LOOKING A BIT BLOATED? CLICK ON THE TOGGLE PIXEL ASPECT RATIO CORRECTION BUTTON. IT'S JUST FOR REFERENCE, BUT IT MAKES YOUR IMAGES LOOK AS IF THEY'RE THE PROPER SHAPE. ELEMENTS SUCH AS TEXT MAY LOOK JAGGED WITH PIXEL ASPECT RATIO CORRECTION TURNED ON. ONCE YOU TURN IT OFF, EVERYTHING WILL BE SHARP ONCE AGAIN.

TEXT ANIMATIONS WITHOUT ANIMATION PRESETS

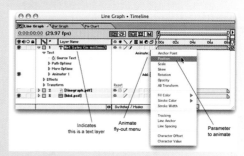

STEP 6: THE NEW TEXT ENGINE INTRODUCED IN AFTER EFFECTS 6.0 ALLOWS YOU TO CREATE AMAZING, DYNAMIC TEXT ANIMATIONS WITH EASE.

1. Type something, then twirl down the text layer.
2. In the Switches column, use the Animate pull-down menu. Choose Position.
3. Twirl down Animator 1, which has just shown up under your text layer.
4. Set position to 1063.0, 0.0. There's no need to set any keyframes for position.
5. Twirl down the range selector. Leave the Start at 0%, but change the End to 35%.
6. Go to the first frame and set a keyframe for Offset with a value of -35%.
7. Go to 2:15 in the Timeline. Set a keyframe for Offset with a value of 100%.
8. Twirl down Advanced.
9. Change "Based on" to Characters Excluding Spaces.
10. Set the amount to -63.
11. Change Shape to Ramp Up.
12. Save.

ANIMATING WITH THE ADVANCED TEXT ENGINE IN AFTER EFFECTS 6.0 AND LATER CAN BE A BIT DIFFICULT AT FIRST; HOWEVER, ONCE YOU GET THE HANG OF IT, YOU CAN UNLEASH YOUR CREATIVITY!

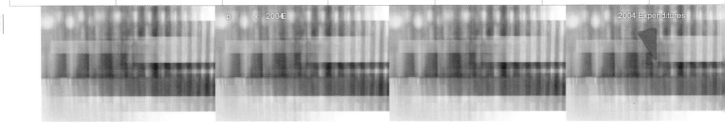

Add the Chart Text

1. Close both Bar Graph and Pie Chart comps and open the Line Graph comp. We'll put the text and numbers on the Line Graph using the Type tool. Make the linegraph.pdf layer visible by clicking the eye icon in the A/V features column. Also, turn on Title Safe. Our text will be just a hair outside of the title-safe area, but it will be fine, so stop worrying.

2. Go to 1:00 in your Timeline. Press the Select the Horizontal Type tool Cmd+T (Ctrl+T) and type over the numbers on the Y-axis, pressing the Return key to create line breaks. Use the Character palette to space your lines. Do not press Return twice to make a larger space; set the leading in the Character palette instead. Use the Paragraphs palette to make your text right-aligned.

3. Apply the same Text Presets as you did in adding the chart title, instead of doing all the work manually. I'm going to show you the quick-and-dirty way to do get your text going quickly.

   a. Twirl down the Net Sales text layer. Select Animator 1 and copy it.
   b. Go to your Y-axis text layer. Twirl down the layer>Text>Animator >Range Selector 1>Advanced.
   c. Change Based On to Lines. Change Shape to Ramp Down.
   d. Press the U key to bring up the Offset keyframes. We need to reverse them. You could just drag them to swap positions, but you can click on the word Offset to highlight it. Choose Animation>Keyframe Assistant>Time Reverse Keyframes.

4. Go to 3:00. Click with the type tool where 1995 begins. This is the X-axis text. To save space, type them as 95, 96, 97, etc. Put only one space between each year; I have a cool trick to space them out. Left-align the paragraph and make your type fit. If you cannot see what you're typing, turn off the visibility for the PDF, or just temporarily turn down the opacity. Remember, single spaces between your years.

5. Twirl down the arrow for the year's text layer and add an animator for Tracking. Twirl down Animator 1. Set the tracking amount

09 » TYPE THE X-AXIS LABELS WITH SINGLE SPACES BETWEEN THEM. USE AN ANIMATOR FOR TRACKING TO SPACE THEM OUT.

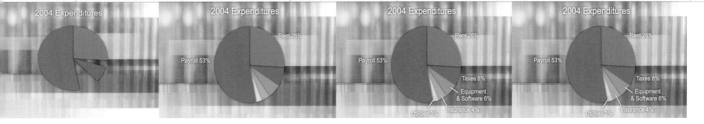

to 25. Twirl down Range Selector. Under Advanced, change the following:

:: Based On: Characters Excluding Spaces
:: Mode: Subtract

6. If they don't quite line up, change the tracking amount. The number will depend upon the font and font size used.

7. Highlight Animator 1. Press Return to make the word editable. Rename it Tracking."

8. You should still have Animator 1 saved to your clipboard (if you don't, go to the Net Sales Text Layer and recopy Animator 1). Paste. Under Advanced, change Based On to Words.

9. Apply the Drop Shadow preset to all of the text. Don't make your text too small. I'd recommend going no less than 18px to be read on a TV.

10. To nudge the size of your text up or down, press Opt+Down Arrow or Opt+Up Arrow (Alt+Down Arrow or Alt+Up Arrow). **(SEE FIGURE 9.)**

11. After you finish your text layers, preview your animation by holding down the Shift key and clicking the RAM Preview button in the Time Control palette. Bring up the Time Control palette by pressing Cmd+3 (Ctrl+3). Drag your text layers around a bit to space them out in time to your liking. Save.

Make the Grid on the Line Graph

Let's make our comp a little easier to work with, shall we?

1. The Shy Layer switch is the Kilroy-looking character in the Switches column. Click the Switches/Modes toggle button to bring up Switches. Select layers that you want to hide and click the Shy Layer box next to one of them. Above the layers, you'll see a larger Shy Layer icon on a button. Click it and watch your layers disappear. Do not fret! By clicking the button again, the layers return. **(SEE FIGURE 10 & 11.)**

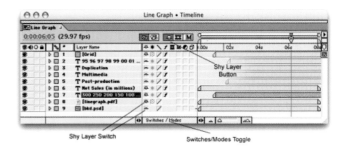

10 » UTILIZING THE SHY LAYER FUNCTION CAN MAKE WORKING WITH STACKS OF LAYERS A BREEZE. YOU MUST ACTIVATE BOTH THE SWITCH AND THE BUTTON TO MAKE A LAYER SHY.

11 » A QUICK WAY TO ACCESS A PREDETERMINED COLOR PALETTE IS TO SELECT IT IN THE PROJECT WINDOW SO THAT YOU CAN SEE THE PREVIEW. WHEN YOU NEED A COLOR, JUST USE THE EYEDROPPER TOOL TO PICK THE HUE YOU NEED. I'VE SET UP A COLOR SCHEME THAT WORKS WITH THE BACKGROUND. CLICK ON COLORSCHEME.PCT IN THE PROJECT WINDOW SO THAT YOU CAN SEE IT IN THE PREVIEW WINDOW. YOU CAN GRAB COLORS FROM THERE WHEN YOU NEED IT.

NEED TO COPY VECTOR FILES FROM ILLUSTRATOR?

To cut and paste from Illustrator to After Effects, your Illustrator preferences need to be set up properly.

In Illustrator, go to Preferences>File Handling & Clipboard. Under Clipboard, check AICB and Preserve Paths.

IF THE FILES & CLIPBOARD PREFERENCES ARE NOT SET UP CORRECTLY IN ILLUS-TRATOR, YOU WILL NOT BE ABLE TO CUT AND PASTE PATHS TO OTHER PROGRAMS.

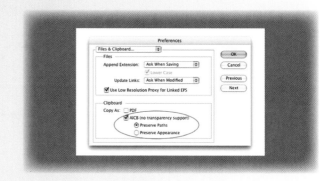

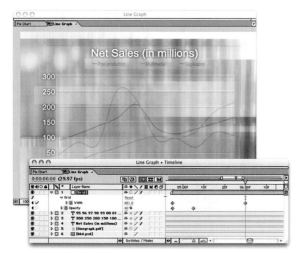

12 » THE GRID EFFECT CAN GIVE YOU SOME COOL WIPE-LIKE EFFECTS WITH THE LINES IF YOU KEYFRAME WIDTH OR HEIGHT.

2. **Make linegraph.pdf visible. Go to 4:25 and create a new solid. Choose Layer>New Solid or press Cmd+Y (Ctrl+Y). Make it 535x275 and name it Grid. Use the eyedropper to pick the lightest shade of blue from colorscheme.pct. Place the solid over the grid in linegraph.pdf.**

3. **Apply the grid filter to the Grid layer (Effect>Render>Grid). Change the following settings for Grid:**

   :: **Anchor: 0, 273 (lower-left corner)**
   :: **Size From: Width and Height sliders**
   :: **Width: 481.0**
   :: **Height 45.5**
   :: **Border: 3**
   :: **Invert Grid: checked**
   :: **Blending Mode: Multiply**

4. **Go to 6:00. Set a keyframe for Width. Go back to the in-point (i) and set Width to 0. Set a keyframe for Opacity with a value of 40%. Select the keyframe and press Shift+Page Down. This moves the keyframe 10 frames ahead. Set the Opacity to 0. In the Switches/Modes column, change the mode to Screen. Save. (SEE FIGURE 12.)**

Animate the Lines on the Line Graph

If you want to be ultra-accurate, you could open linegraph.pdf in Illustrator, do a little surgery on the lines, and then copy and paste them onto solids in After Effects. Trust me, it's a lot of work. We're going to simplify things by drawing the lines with the Pen tool in After Effects.

1. **Make all layers shy. Go to 6:15. Create a new solid and click the Make Comp Size button. Call it Line Postproduction. Duplicate this layer twice, naming the duplicates Line Multimedia and Line Duplication. Turn off the visibility for Line Multimedia and Line Duplication.**

2. **Set the opacity of the Line Postproduction layer to 0. Grab that**

Pen tool (G) and trace the Postproduction line. Draw the Multimedia and Duplication on their respective layers. Save. **(SEE FIGURE 13.)**

3. Go to 7:15 and press Opt+M to set a keyframe for the mask. Jump back to 6:29. If you don't like the default yellow of the mask, press the M key. You'll see a yellow box next to the words Mask 1. Click on the yellow and the color picker will pop up. Change the color.

4. Select only the Line Postproduction layer. Use the Pen tool to draw at the point where the line starts and end at the end of the graph. If you hold down the Shift key as you draw the line, the line will stay perfectly level. You want to be careful not to continue the path of the existing mask, so if the Pen tool icon suddenly has a plus sign next to it, move the pen down a few pixels before you click. When you're finished, Option-click the line to select it and use the arrow keys to nudge it into place

5. Press the M key to bring up Mask 1 and Mask 2. Set a keyframe for Mask 2. Select and copy the keyframe. Select Mask 1's mask shape. Make Paste, then delete Mask 2.

6. Repeat Step 10 with the Line Multiplication and Line Duplication line layers.

Add the Stroke to the Lines

1. Set the opacity back to 100% for all three line layers. Select Line Postproduction, and add a Stroke (Effect>Render>Stroke). Use the following settings:

    :: Path: Mask 1
    :: Color: Blue
    :: Brush Hardness: 100%
    :: Paint Style: On Transparent
    :: Leave the other settings as is.

2. Let's animate the line a bit more, drawing on the line from the center, into the straight line. Simply animate the Start and End settings in the Stroke effect.

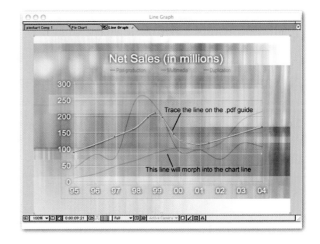

13 » THE LINE WILL MORPH FROM A STRAIGHT LINE INTO THE MOUNTAINOUS LINE OF THE CHART.

GO TO TIME

If you're on a laptop, you may not be able to use certain shortcuts, like function keys and Page Up and Page Down to move through the Timeline. You can use the Cmd+G (Ctrl+G) shortcut to bring up the Go To Time dialog box.

» WANT TO GO TO 0:00:04:00? INSTEAD OF TYPING ALL THOSE ZEROS IN THE GO TO TIME BOX, YOU CAN JUST TYPE "4." (THAT'S 4 WITH A PERIOD AFTER IT).

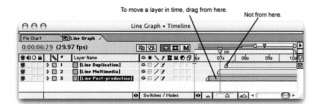

14 » STEP 7: WHEN DRAGGING LAYERS IN THE TIMELINE, HOLD DOWN YOUR MOUSE BUTTON AS YOU DRAG, GRABBING THE COLORED PORTION OF THE BAR. DO NOT GRAB THE LAYER HANDLE.

3. Go to 7:13 in the Timeline and set keyframes for both Start and End. Jump back to 6:29, the in-point of the layer, and set both of the values of Start and End to 50%.

4. Preview. Pretty swell, eh!

5. This same effect will need to be applied to Duplication and Multimedia. Follow the instructions in Adding the Chart Title above to save the effect as an Animation Preset. Call it Chart Stroke and save it in the Charts folder that you created.

6. Apply the Chart Stroke preset to Line Multimedia and Line Duplication. Open up the Stroke effect and change the color of the lines. The Multimedia line needs to be green and the Duplication line blue.

7. Set the Opacity back to 100%. Stagger the times of the layers so that Line Multimedia begins at 6:29 and Line Duplication begins at 7:08. (SEE FIGURE 14.)

8. Turn off the visibility of linegraph.pdf and save.

Make the Key for the Line Graph

1. Go to 5:00. Use the Type tool to add the text across the top. Type "Postproduction" in white 16px Arial, which is about the smallest that I would advise for text that you want to be read on a television screen.

2. Jump to 5:10 by holding down the Shift key and pressing Page Down. Press the T key to bring up opacity. Set a keyframe for 100 percent. Jump back to 5:00 by holding down the Shift key and pressing Page Up. Set the value of Opacity to 0 percent. Apply that good old Charts Drop shadow preset to the layer.

3. The quickest way to make the other words in the key is to duplicate Postproduction twice, move the new layers to the right, and type the words "Multimedia" and "Duplication" over it. Drag Multimedia to start at 5:10 and Duplication at 5:20.

4. Go to 5:10. To make the key, create a new solid called Key Post-

GET ACCURATE SPACING BY USING THE ALIGN & DISTRIBUTE TOOL

Get accurate spacing by using the Align & Distribute Tool

» YOU'LL RECOGNIZE THE ALIGN PALETTE FROM ILLUSTRATOR AND PHOTOSHOP. USE IT TO ACCURATELY ALIGN YOUR TEXT OR DISTRIBUTE IT EVENLY.

production. Set the Opacity to 0%. Use the Pen tool to create a short line to the left of the word Postproduction. Apply the Stroke Animation preset. Turn the Opacity back up to 100%. **(SEE FIGURE 15.)**

5. Duplicate Key Postproduction twice. Rename the layers Key Multimedia and Key Duplication. Nudge them so that they line up with the corresponding text by holding down the Shift key and pressing the right arrow key repeatedly. Holding down the Shift key will let you move in increments of 10 pixels instead of one pixel.

6. On both layers, change the color of the stroke so that it matches the color of the corresponding line in the graph. Move Key Multimedia in the Timeline so that it starts at 5:20 and move Key Duplication to 6:00.

15 » STEP 4: TO MAKE THE KEY, DRAW A SHORT LINE WITH THE PEN TOOL AND USE THE CHART STROKE ANIMATION PRESET THAT YOU CREATED.

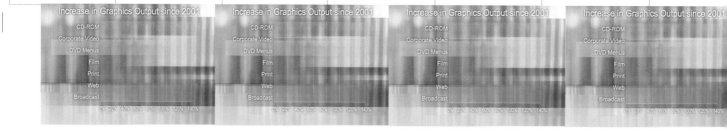

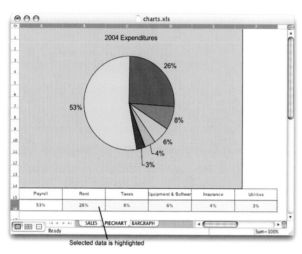

16 » YOU CAN EASILY RECREATE A PIE CHART IN ILLUSTRATOR BY PASTING THE DATA
COPIED FROM EXCEL INTO THE ILLUSTRATOR'S GRAPH TOOL.

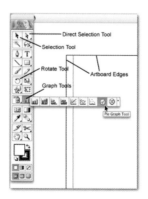

17 » STEP 4: IN ILLUSTRATOR, CHOOSE THE PIE GRAPH TOOL IN THE GRAPH TOOLS.
THE SELECTION AND ROTATE TOOLS ARE OTHER TOOLS THAT YOU WILL USE.

Preparing the Pie Chart in Illustrator

You could cut and paste the whole pie chart, but it's actually easier to make a new graph in Illustrator by pasting the data. (SEE FIGURE 16.)

1. Launch Excel. Open the Pie Chart workbook tab.

2. Select the line of data in the spreadsheet. Copy.

3. In Illustrator, create a new document (640x480, landscape orientation, RGB Color). Call it Pie Chart.

4. Select the Pie Graph tool. (SEE FIGURE 17.)

5. Draw a box with the crosshairs. Your pie chart needs to be perfectly round, so hold down the Shift key as you draw your pie chart with the crosshairs to constrain proportions. The circle should fill about half of the height of the work area.

6. In the chart data area, select the top left cell and paste.

7. You'll need to remove the percent symbol from each of the cells. Luckily, there are only a few. To delete them, choose each cell individually and delete the percent symbol from the data entry line across the top. (SEE FIGURE 18.)

8. Click the checkmark in the upper-right corner to apply your data.

9. Select the pie chart with the Selection tool. Use the Rotate tool (R) to rotate 178°, matching the angle of the original.

10. Each piece of the pie needs to be put on its own layer, so ungroup (Object>Ungroup). A pop-up message appears: "The selection contains a graph. After a graph is ungrouped you will no longer be able to access its graph style, its data or change its graph designs." Click OK.

11. Ungroup three more times by pressing Cmd+Shift+G (Ctrl+Shift+G) until the layer is broken into paths. Twirl down the arrow next to the layer to see whether it is broken into paths. (SEE FIGURE 19.)

12. Select Layer 1 in the Layers palette. In the fly-out menu on the upper right of the Layers palette, choose Release to Layers (Sequence).

13. The pieces of the pie are now on their own layers. Select all of the pieces of the pie. Hold down the Shift key and drag them above Layer 1 in the Layers palette. The cursor will be come a fist, grabbing your layers.

14. Label your layers by double-clicking a layer and changing the name. Call them Payroll, Rent, etc. View the original Excel document or your hard copy for reference.

15. Save it as piechart.ai. To ensure that the file displays correctly in After Effects, select the Create PDF Compatible File option in the Illustrator Native Format Options dialog box.

16. Leave it in grayscale. We'll add the colors in After Effects. **(SEE FIGURE 19.)**

Make the Pie

1. Open your After Effects project file. Import piechart.ai as a composition. The original comp called Pie Chart is in the Project window, along with a comp and folder titled piechart Comp 1. The folder contains all of the pieces of the pie. The comp is the whole pie.

2. Double-click Pie Chart Comp 1 to open it. It needs to be 10 seconds long, so if it is not, change your Composition Settings by pressing Cmd+K (Ctrl+K).

3. We'll animate the pieces in this comp and then nest this comp inside of the Pie Chart comp. Delete Layer 1 and change the background color by pressing Cmd+B (Ctrl+B) so you can see the pie pieces easily.

4. Select Payroll. Apply a Radial Wipe (Effect>Transition>Radial Wipe). Go to 0:00. Set the Start Angle to 0 x −195. Set a keyframe for Transition of 61%. Go to 0:15. Set a keyframe for Transition Complete of 0%.

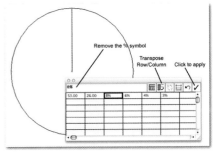

18 » STEP 7: PASTE THE DATA FROM EXCEL INTO THE CHART DATA BOX. ONLY NUMERICAL DATA IS ALLOWED, SO THE PERCENT SYMBOLS WILL NEED TO BE DELETED.

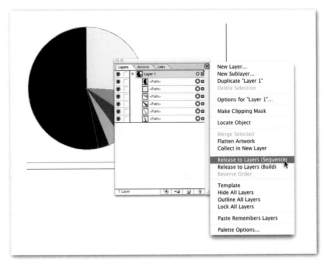

19 » STEP 11: UNGROUP UNTIL LAYER 1 IS BROKEN INTO PATHS, THEN RELEASE TO LAYERS (SEQUENCE).

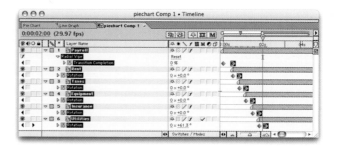

20 » APPLY EASY EASE IN TO YOUR ELEMENTS FOR A SMOOTHER, MORE NATURAL MOTION.

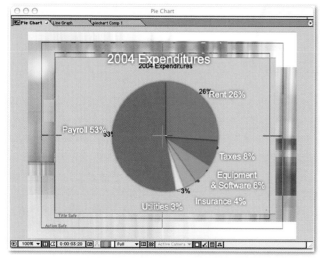

21 » PLACE THE TEXT AROUND THE PIE SO IT DOES NOT LOOK TOO CROWDED.

5. Jump to 0:25. Select all the layers except Payroll. Shift+click the layers to select multiple files. Press Cmd+[(Ctrl+[) to set a new in-point for all of the layers. Press Option+R to set a keyframe for rotation on all selected layers.

6. Go to 0:15. These layers need to hide behind the Payroll layer. Set the rotation value to 169° for each of the five layers by selecting all five and setting one of them to 169°.

7. Select all layers and press the U key. You'll see keyframes for the Radial Wipe Transition Completion on the Payroll layer, and Rotation keyframes on the other layers. Select only the second keyframe on each layer. Press Shift+F9 to add an Easy Ease In (or choose Animation>Keyframe Assistant>Easy Ease In). This will make the motion flow better. Preview and save. (**SEE FIGURE 20.**)

8. Stagger out the layers so that the layers are 10 frames apart in sequence. Rent starts at 0:25, Taxes at 1:05, Equipment at 1:15, Insurance at 1:25 and Utilities at 2:05.

9. Click on Payroll and add a Fill (Effect>Render>Fill). Set the color to the spicy mustard color in the upper right of colorscheme.pct. Apply Fill to the remaining pie pieces, choosing nice shades from colorscheme.pct.

10. Apply the Charts Drop Shadow preset to all of the pie pieces. Close the Comp window by pressing Cmd+W (Ctrl+W).

Finish Up the Pie Chart

1. Open Pie Chart comp. Drag Pie Chart Comp 1 into the Pie Chart comp. Make sure it starts at 1:20. Center the pie chart in the Comp Window. If it doesn't look round, remember the Pixel Aspect Ratio Correction button on the Comp window.

2. I scaled the pie to 77%. Your pie chart may be a different size, so scale it as you see appropriate. It should be slightly larger than the pie chart in the PDF guide.

3. The pie chart has percentages but no indicators of what the

numbers refer to. You can refer to the original Excel document for the information or your printout.

4. Instead of making the text shuffle on, a simple fade in over ten frames will do the trick. Go to 4:00 and type Payroll 53%. Make it white, Arial, 20px and apply the Animation Preset for Charts Drop Shadow. Position it to the left of the Payroll piece of the pie, which is the largest.

5. Jump to 4:10 and set a keyframe for Opacity. Back at 4:00, set Opacity to 0%. Select the second keyframe and apply Easy Ease In.

6. Duplicate the text layer "Payroll 53%" by pressing Cmd+D five times. Move ahead in the Timeline to see the text. Drag the copies to their positions and then type over them with the correct text. If your text looks jaggy, you're viewing at a lower resolution or Pixel Aspect Ratio Correction is turned on. It is clean, so put your worries aside. **(SEE FIGURE 21.)**

7. Use Option+Shift+Page Down to nudge a layer 10 frames later.

   :: Payroll starts at 4:00
   :: Rent starts at 4:10
   :: Taxes starts at 4:20
   :: Equipment starts at 5:00
   :: Insurance starts at 5:10
   :: Utilities starts at 5:20

8. At 5:20, add the lines between the pie and the type. Create a new solid. Click the Make Comp Size button and call it Lines. Set the Opacity to 0% so you can see what you're doing. Use the Pen tool to draw short lines from the text to the corresponding pie piece for Equipment, Insurance and Utilities. They will animate in a quirky fun way, some starting at the pie and others starting at the text. **(SEE FIGURE 22.)**

9. Go to the in-point of the Lines layer. Set the Opacity back to 100%. Apply the Stroke Animation Preset that you made for the Line Graph. Twirl down Stroke and set All Masks to On. Stroke Sequentially should also be on. Change the color to white.

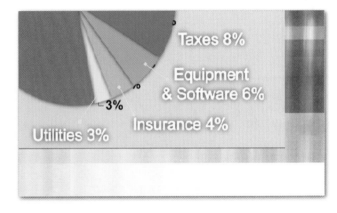

22 » USE THE PEN TOOL TO DRAW THREE SEPARATE LINES THAT RUN BETWEEN THE TEXT AND THE CORRESPONDING PIE PIECE. APPLY THE STROKE ANIMATION PRESET THAT YOU CREATED EARLIER.

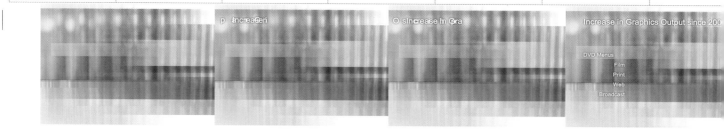

10. Apply the Charts Drop Shadow preset to the lines. Turn off the visibility for piechart.pdf, save, and preview. Two down, one to go.

Speeding Your Way Through the Bar Graph

1. Open the Bar Graph comp. You should see three layers: bkd. psd, bargraph.pdf, and the title, centered across the top of the screen.

2. Open the Line Graph comp. Select and copy the X and Y axis labels and Grid.

3. Press Shift+, (comma) to tab back to the bar graph. Go to 1:00 and paste. (SEE FIGURE 23.)

23 » STEP 16: SELECT THE LAYERS IN THE LINE GRAPH COMP TO REPURPOSE THEM IN THE BAR GRAPH.

4. Scale and position the Grid to fit. I scaled it to X=70%, Y=98%. Hit the i key to go to the In Point, then press the U key to bring up all keyframes. Set the Opacity to 100% so that you can see the grid.

5. Click the stopwatch next to Height and Width to delete the keyframes. Jump ahead to 6:00 and set Width to 69.0. Set a keyframe for Height to 273.0. Jump back to 4:25 and set Height to 0. Set Opacity to 0% at the first frame.

6. Nudge the position of the X and Y axis Text layers to line up with the text on the PDF guide. Use the Character palette to adjust the leading of the Y-axis text. Type over the numbers with the correct text. Instead of typing CD-ROM Graphics, just type CD-ROM.

7. Notice that Corporate Video doesn't quite fit. Instead of making the text smaller, move everything 50px to the right. The title and background can stay where they are. Unlock bargraph.pdf. Select bargraph.pdf, Grid, and the Y-axis and Y-axis text. Press Shift+Right Arrow five times. Lock bargraph.pdf. (SEE FIGURE 24.)

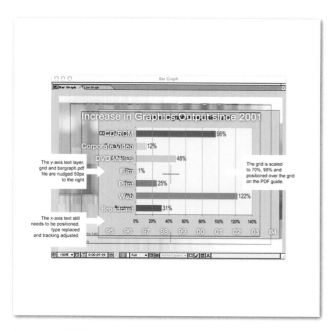

24 » STEP 16: NUDGING THE PDF GUIDE LAYER, THE GRID, AND THE X AND Y AXIS LABELS HELPS EVERYTHING FIT ON SCREEN.

8. On the X-axis, type the percentages over top of the years. Put just one space between the numbers. Remember that Tracking Animator that you added to the text on the Line Graph? You copied that too. In the Character palette, set the font size to 18px and the horizontal scale to 85%. Left-align the text with the

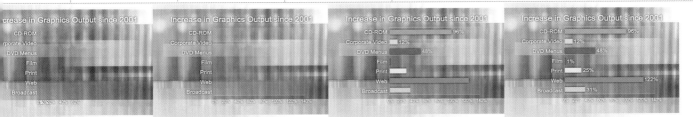

text on bargraph.pdf. Twirl down the layer Text Tracking. Set the Tracking Amount to 11, or whatever works with your font. Twirl the layer closed.

Animate the Bars

There are about a thousand ways to animate these bars, so I've chosen a simple method.

1. Select colorscheme.pct in the Project window so that you can see it in the Preview window.

2. The Web bar is the longest, so let's start there. At 6:00, create a new solid, 256x20. Call it Web. Use the color picker to pick the shade from the colorscheme.pct file in the Preview window. Press A to bring up Anchor Point. Set the Anchor Point to 0.0, 10.0. Line up the line with the Web bar on the PDF guide.

3. Jump to 8:00 and press Option+S to set a keyframe for Scale. Go to 6:00 and set Scale to 0 percent. Select the second keyframe and press Shift+F9, Easy Ease In. Set Opacity to 50 percent.

4. Go to 6:15 and duplicate Web six times. Line up the solids with the PDF guide. Open the Composition Setting and change the names and colors. Put the bars in order in the Timeline. (SEE FIGURE 25.)

5. We need to keep the bars growing at the same speed, so I've got a little trick. Go to 6:00. Select all six bar layers. Press the S key to bring up the Scale keyframes. Start with Film, since it's the shortest. At 6:01, the Film bar is as long as it needs to be. Set a keyframe at 6:01. Delete the keyframe at 8:00 for Film.

6. The next shortest bar is Corporate Video. Press Page Down until the bar is the right length. At 6:05, they match up, so set a Scale keyframe for Corporate Video and delete the keyframe at 8:00.

7. Now, the Print bar. At 6:10, the length matches. Set a keyframe for Scale and delete the keyframe at 8:00.

8. Repeat the process with the remaining bars.

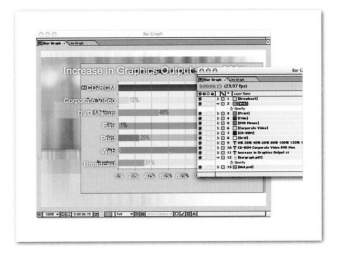

25 » DUPLICATE THE LONGEST BAR AND DISTRIBUTE THEM. YOU CAN USE THE ALIGN TOOL FOR ACCURACY.

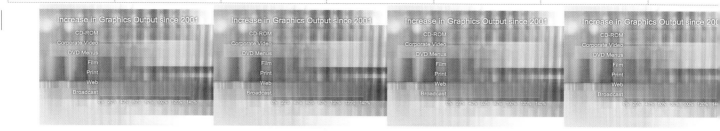

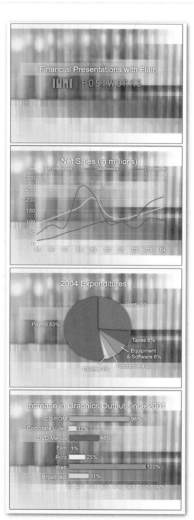

26 » THE FINISHED GRAPHS AND SHOW OPEN.

9. Select all six bars and press the T key. Change the opacity of one of the layers to 100%, and they'll all change. While the layers are still selected, apply the Charts Drop Shadow preset to help them pop.

10. Now, we'll add the percent numbers at the end of the bars. We're going to cheat again and copy text from the pie chart. Open the Pie Chart comp. Select and copy "Utilities 3%."

11. Switch back to the Bar Graph comp. Go to 7:15. Paste. Drag it over the "96%" on the PDF guide layer and type "96%" over it.

12. Duplicate the 96% layer, place it where it needs to go, change the number. When you're finished, stagger the in-points of the layers so that 96% starts at 7:15, 12% starts at 7:25, DVD Menus starts at 8:05, and so on.

13. Turn off bargraph.pdf. You're finished with all three graphs! Save.

Building a Quick Open

1. Create a new comp that is 720x480, D1 NTSC. Make it 4:00 in duration and call it Open Animation. Drag bkd.psd into the comp.

2. Open Bar Graph and copy the title to your clipboard. Go back to the Open Animation comp and paste at the first frame. Go ahead a few seconds so that you can see the text. Type "Financials with Flair" over the title. Nudge the layer down to about the lower third of the screen.

3. Go to 2:15. Drag postworks-logo.psd, already imported for you and in the Elements folder, into the Timeline. Center it on screen. Apply Charts Drop Shadow. (SEE FIGURE 26.)

Putting It All Together

1. Render all of the movies at the best quality possible for your DVD authoring program. It is best to render to a lossless codec such as animation. you can then compress to MPEG2. Starting with a high-quality file will result in smaller compressions with better image quality.

2. Import the Open Animation and three graphs into your DVD authoring program. The idea is to put them in order—Open, Line Graph, Pie Chart, and Bar Graph. Program a Next button so that the speaker can go to the next chart when he is ready. Each movie will hold on the final frame so that the graphic or chart will remain on-screen as long as is needed.

3. Ideally, you would have a moving background and some transitions between slides, so you can do that on your own.

ABOUT THE AUTHOR

When Michele Yamazaki was a child she was a huge fan of Top 40 and always wanted to work in radio. In college, she worked on a degree in broadcast and had to take video classes. After Video Editing 1, she was hooked.

In 1995, she interned at a company called Postworks, a post-production and Communications Company. Some of the high-profile projects she has worked on are the current graphics package for the Jerry Springer Show and the animation for the big screen of the last AC/DC world tour. She spends most of her time at the company working on web site development.

In 2001, she launched the AE FreeMart with Roland Kahlenberg. In 2002, she started the West Michigan After Effects User Group with Matt Schirado, a friend and editor at a local TV station.

In 2003, her life changed. Her husband, Max, and she had a baby named Lily. It was a tough pregnancy and she had to spend 80 days in the hospital on bed rest. During that time, her priorities became refocused on her family. Lily is now a happy, healthy two-year-old.

Michele went back to work part-time at Postworks. In 2004 she was offered a teaching position at Kendall College of Art and Design, teaching After Effects and Photoshop.

Not long after that, Toolfarm asked her to join their team as web designer and content creator. She is still at Postworks and Kendall. She's busy but is having a blast.